PRACTICE - ASSESS - DIAGNOSE

180 Days of WRITING for First Grade

Author
Jodene Smith, M.A.

Shell Education

Standards

For information on how this resource meets national and other state standards, see pages 4–6. You may also review this information by scanning the QR code or visiting our website at http://www.shelleducation.com and following the on-screen directions.

Publishing Credits

Corinne Burton, M.A.Ed., *President*; Emily R. Smith, M.A.Ed., *Content Director*; Jennifer Wilson, *Editor*; Grace Alba Le, *Multimedia Designer*; Don Tran, *Production Artist*; Stephanie Bernard, *Assistant Editor*; Amber Goff, *Editorial Assistant*

Image Credits

pp. 91, 110, 127, 211–212, 214: iStock; All other images Shutterstock

Standards

Shell Education
5482 Argosy Avenue
Huntington Beach, CA 92649-1030
www.tcmpub.com/shell-education

ISBN 978-1-4258-1524-0

TABLE OF CONTENTS

INTRODUCTION

The Need for Practice

To be successful in today's writing classrooms, students must deeply understand both concepts and procedures so that they can discuss and demonstrate their understanding. Demonstrating understanding is a process that must be continually practiced for students to be successful. Practice is especially important to help students apply their concrete, conceptual understanding of each particular writing skill.

Understanding Assessment

In addition to providing opportunities for frequent practice, teachers must be able to assess students' writing skills. This is important so that teachers can adequately address students' misconceptions, build on their current understandings, and challenge them appropriately. Assessment is a long-term process that involves careful analysis of student responses from a discussion, project, practice sheet, or test. When analyzing the data, it is important for teachers to reflect on how their teaching practices may have influenced students' responses and to identify those areas where additional instruction may be required. In short, the data gathered from assessments should be used to inform instruction: slow down, speed up, or reteach. This type of assessment is called *formative assessment.*

HOW TO USE THIS BOOK *(cont.)*

Overarching Themes	Weekly Themes	Standards
Great Americans	**Week 19:** Dr. Martin Luther King Jr. **Week 20:** George Washington	**Writing 1.2**—Write informative/explanatory texts in which they name a topic, supply some facts about the topic, and provide some sense of closure.
People We Love	**Week 21:** Family **Week 22:** Friends	**Writing 1.3**—Write narratives in which they recount two or more appropriately sequenced events, include some details regarding what happened, use temporal words to signal event order, and provide some sense of closure.
Round Things to Eat	**Week 23:** Pie **Week 24:** Pizza	**Writing 1.1**—Write opinion pieces in which they introduce the topic or name the book they are writing about, state an opinion, supply a reason for the opinion, and provide some sense of closure.
Things in the Sky	**Week 25:** Airplanes **Week 26:** Kites	**Writing 1.3**—Write narratives in which they recount two or more appropriately sequenced events, include some details regarding what happened, use temporal words to signal event order, and provide some sense of closure.
Growth and Change	**Week 27:** Animals **Week 28:** Plants	**Writing 1.2**—Write informative/explanatory texts in which they name a topic, supply some facts about the topic, and provide some sense of closure.
Then and Now	**Week 29:** Transportation **Week 30:** Technology	**Writing 1.3**—Write narratives in which they recount two or more appropriately sequenced events, include some details regarding what happened, use temporal words to signal event order, and provide some sense of closure.
Things with Wings	**Week 31:** Butterflies **Week 32:** Birds	**Writing 1.2**—Write informative/explanatory texts in which they name a topic, supply some facts about the topic, and provide some sense of closure.
American Symbols	**Week 33:** Statue of Liberty **Week 34:** The Flag	**Writing 1.2**—Write informative/explanatory texts in which they name a topic, supply some facts about the topic, and provide some sense of closure.
Signs of Summer	**Week 35:** The Beach **Week 36:** Vacation	**Writing 1.3**—Write narratives in which they recount two or more appropriately sequenced events, include some details regarding what happened, use temporal words to signal event order, and provide some sense of closure.

HOW TO USE THIS BOOK *(cont.)*

Weekly Setup

Write each prompt on the board throughout the appropriate week. Students should reference the prompts as they work through the activity pages so that they stay focused on the topics and the right genre of writing: opinion, informative/explanatory, and narrative. You may wish to print copies of this chart from the digital resources (filename: G1_writingprompts.pdf) and distribute them to students to keep throughout the school year.

Week	Prompt
1	Write about going back to school. Tell why you do or do not like it.
2	Write about your favorite teacher. Tell why you like him or her.
3	Write about health workers. Include at least one fact.
4	Write about safety helpers. Include at least one fact.
5	Write about an apple. Include at least one fact.
6	Write about a pumpkin. Include at least one of its parts.
7	Do you like monsters? Tell why you do or do not like them.
8	What is your favorite candy? Write about it, and tell why you like it.
9	Write about a time you played soccer. What did you do? Who did you play with?
10	Write about a time you saw a basketball game. What did you do? What did you see?
11	Write about a time you saw a hibernating animal.

Week	Prompt
12	Write about a time you dressed in winter clothing.
13	Do you think it is fun to bake gingerbread men? Tell why or why not.
14	What is you favorite winter celebration? Tell how you celebrate. Give reasons why it is your favorite.
15	Is it fun to celebrate New Year's? Write about why you do or do not think it is fun.
16	Do you like to celebrate Chinese New Year? Write about why you do or do not like to celebrate.
17	Do you think building a snowman is fun? Write about why you do or do not think it is fun.
18	What is your favorite winter sport? Write about the sport. Give reasons why it is your favorite.
19	Write about Dr. Martin Luther King Jr. Include at least one fact.
20	Write about George Washington. Include at least one fact.
21	Write about a time you spent with family. Give details about how you spent your time together.

HOW TO USE THIS BOOK *(cont.)*

Week	Prompt
22	Write about an activity you did with a friend. Give details about the activity you did.
23	Do you think apple pie is the best pie? Tell why you do or do not think it is the best.
24	Write about your favorite kind of pizza. Why is it your favorite?
25	Write about a time you flew on an airplane. Tell about where you went and who you were with. If you have not flown on an airplane, write about what you think it would be like.
26	Write about a time you flew a kite. Include two events.
27	Write about hens. Include at least one fact.
28	Write about how a plant grows. Include at least one fact.
29	Write about a time you went on a vacation with your family. What type of transportation did you use to get there? Include at least two details.
30	Write about a time you used technology. Include at least two details.
31	Write about butterflies. Include at least one fact.
32	Write about birds. Include at least one fact.
33	Write about the Statue of Liberty. Include at least one fact.
34	Write about your country's flag. Include at least one fact.

Week	Prompt
35	Write about a time you went to the beach. Include where you were, who you were with, and what you did.
36	Write about a vacation you went on. Include where you went, who you were with, and what you did.

HOW TO USE THIS BOOK *(cont.)*

Using the Practice Pages

The activity pages provide practice and assessment opportunities for each day of the school year. Teachers may wish to prepare packets of weekly practice pages for the classroom or for homework. As outlined on pages 5–6, each two-week unit is aligned to one writing standard. **Note:** Before implementing each week's activity pages, review the corresponding prompt on pages 7–8 with students and have students brainstorm thoughts about each topic.

On odd weeks, students practice the daily skills using mentor texts. On even weeks, students use what they have learned in the previous week and apply it to their own writing.

Each day focuses on one of the steps in the writing process: prewriting, drafting, revising, editing, and publishing. **Note:** Distribute the *Editing Marks* on page 207 to students. They can reference this page as they work through the weeks. Alternatively, you can reproduce it poster sized and hang it in your classroom.

There are 18 overarching themes. Each odd week and the following even week focus on unique themes that fit under one overarching theme. For a list of the overarching themes and individual weekly themes, see pages 5–6.

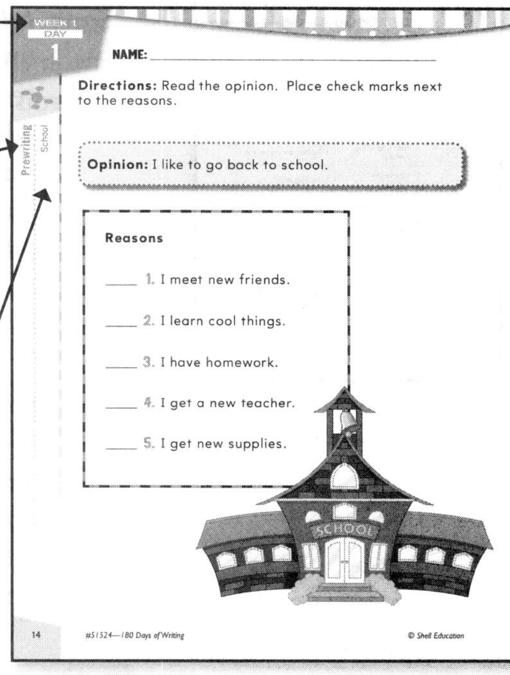
WEEK 1 DAY 1

NAME: ____

Prewriting School

Directions: Read the opinion. Place check marks next to the reasons.

Opinion: I like to go back to school.

Reasons

____ 1. I meet new friends.

____ 2. I learn cool things.

____ 3. I have homework.

____ 4. I get a new teacher.

____ 5. I get new supplies.

14 #51524—180 Days of Writing © Shell Education

Rubrics for the three genres of writing (opinion, informative/explanatory, and narrative) can be found on pages 200–202. Be sure to share these rubrics with students often so that they know what is expected of them.

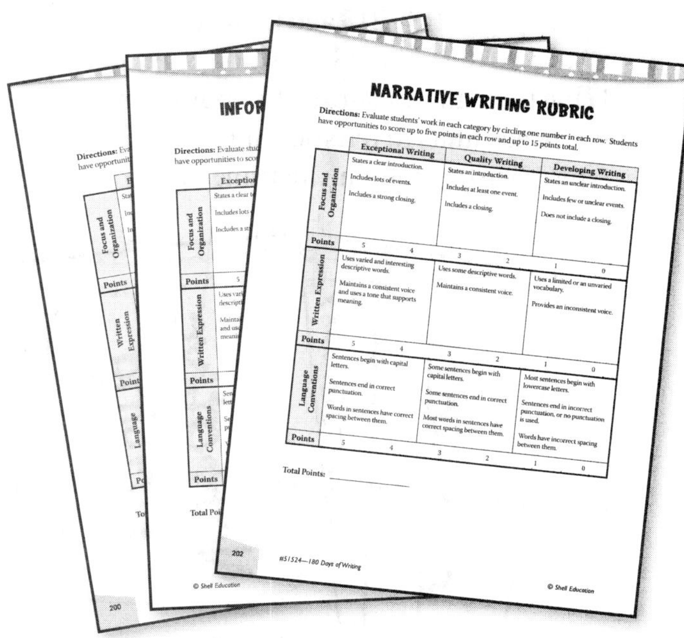
NARRATIVE WRITING RUBRIC

Directions: Evaluate students' work in each category by circling one number in each row. Students have opportunities to score up to five points in each row and up to 15 points total.

	Exceptional Writing	Quality Writing	Developing Writing
Focus and Organization	States a clear introduction. Includes lots of events. Includes a strong closing.	States an introduction. Includes at least one event. Includes a closing.	States an unclear introduction. Includes few or unclear events. Does not include a closing.
Points	5 4	3 2	1 0
Written Expression	Uses varied and interesting descriptive words. Maintains a consistent voice and uses a tone that supports meaning.	Uses some descriptive words. Maintains a consistent voice.	Uses a limited or an unvaried vocabulary. Provides an inconsistent voice.
Points	5 4	3 2	1 0
Language Conventions	Sentences begin with capital letters. Sentences end in correct punctuation. Words in sentences have correct spacing between them.	Some sentences begin with capital letters. Some sentences end in correct punctuation. Most words in sentences have correct spacing between them.	Most sentences begin with lowercase letters. Sentences end in incorrect punctuation, or no punctuation is used. Words have incorrect spacing between them.
Points	5 4	3 2	1 0

Total Points: ____

202 #51524—180 Days of Writing © Shell Education

HOW TO USE THIS BOOK *(cont.)*

Using the Results to Differentiate Instruction

Once results are gathered and analyzed, teachers can use the results to inform the way they differentiate instruction. The data can help determine which writing types are the most difficult for students and which students need additional instructional support and continued practice.

Whole-Class Support

The results of the diagnostic analysis may show that the entire class is struggling with a particular writing genre. If these concepts have been taught in the past, this indicates that further instruction or reteaching is necessary. If these concepts have not been taught in the past, this data is a great preassessment and may demonstrate that students do not have a working knowledge of the concepts. Thus, careful planning for the length of the unit(s) or lesson(s) must be considered, and additional front-loading may be required.

Small-Group or Individual Support

The results of the diagnostic analysis may show that an individual student or a small group of students is struggling with a particular writing genre. If these concepts have been taught in the past, this indicates that further instruction or reteaching is necessary. Consider pulling these students aside while others are working independently to instruct them further on the concept(s). Students may also benefit from extra practice using games or computer-based resources. Teachers can also use the results to help identify individual students or groups of proficient students who are ready for enrichment or above-grade-level instruction. These students may benefit from independent learning contracts or more challenging activities.

Digital Resources

Reference page 215 for information about accessing the digital resources and an overview of the contents.

STANDARDS CORRELATIONS

Shell Education is committed to producing educational materials that are research and standards based. In this effort, we have correlated all of our products to the academic standards of all 50 states, the District of Columbia, the Department of Defense Dependents Schools, and all Canadian provinces.

How to Find Standards Correlations

To print a customized correlation report of this product for your state, visit our website at **www.tcmpub.com/shell-education** and follow the on-screen directions. If you require assistance in printing correlation reports, please contact our Customer Service Department at 1-877-777-3450.

Purpose and Intent of Standards

Legislation mandates that all states adopt academic standards that identify the skills students will learn in kindergarten through grade twelve. Many states also have standards for Pre-K. This same legislation sets requirements to ensure the standards are detailed and comprehensive.

Standards are designed to focus instruction and guide adoption of curricula. Standards are statements that describe the criteria necessary for students to meet specific academic goals. They define the knowledge, skills, and content students should acquire at each level. Standards are also used to develop standardized tests to evaluate students' academic progress.

Teachers are required to demonstrate how their lessons meet state standards. State standards are used in the development of all of our products, so educators can be assured they meet the academic requirements of each state.

The activities in this book are aligned to today's national and state-specific college and career readiness standards. The chart on page 4 lists the writing and language standards used throughout this book. A more detailed chart on pages 5–6 correlates the specific writing standards to each week.

NAME: ______________________________

Directions: Read the opinion. Place check marks next to the reasons.

Opinion: I like to go back to school.

Reasons

_____ **1.** I meet new friends.

_____ **2.** I learn cool things.

_____ **3.** I have homework.

_____ **4.** I get a new teacher.

_____ **5.** I get new supplies.

NAME: ______________________________

Directions: Read the text. Then, underline each sentence in green, red, or blue.

Green:	**Red:**	**Blue:**
opinion	detail	closure

I like to go back to school. I get a new teacher. I get a new backpack. I see school friends again. I look forward to going back to school.

Printing Practice

Directions: Trace the word. Write it on your own.

school

NAME: ______________________________

Directions: Read the sentences. They say the same thing. Circle the sentences that sound best to you.

1. I like to go back to school.

   Going back to school is fun.

2. I get a new teacher.

   My teacher is new.

3. I get a new backpack.

   Mom buys me a new backpack.

4. I look forward to going back to school.

   Going back to school is something I look forward to.

NAME: ____

Directions: Add periods to the sentences.

1. Going back to school is fun
2. My teacher is new
3. I see school friends again
4. Mom buys me a new backpack
5. I meet new friends

Boost Your Learning!

Every sentence has to have an ending mark.

NAME: ________________________________

Directions: Read the text. Draw a picture to match. Then, fill in the checklist.

Going back to school is fun. My teacher is new. I see school friends again. Mom buys me a new backpack. I look forward to going back to school.

Checklist ☑

- ❑ Sentences begin with capital letters.
- ❑ Sentences end with punctuation.
- ❑ There are spaces between words.

NAME: ____________________

Directions: Draw your favorite teacher. State your opinion. Then, write reasons why you like him or her.

Opinion

I like ____________________.

Reasons

NAME: ________________________________

Directions: Write about your favorite teacher. Then, fill in the checklist.

Opinion

My favorite teacher is ________________________________

________________________________.

Reasons

I like him/her because ________________________________

____

________________________________.

Closing Sentence

____

is my favorite teacher.

Checklist ☑

- ❑ I state an opinion.
- ❑ I have a detail.
- ❑ I have a closing.

NAME: ______________________________

Directions: Read the sentences. Revise the sentences to say the same things in different ways.

1. **Sentence:** First grade is what grade she teaches.

   Revised: She teaches ______________________.

2. **Sentence:** The boy gets help from the teacher.

   Revised: The teacher helps ______________________.

3. **Sentence:** Math is her favorite subject.

   Revised: Her favorite subject ______________________.

NAME: ______________________________

Directions: Circle the pictures that have to do with health workers.

mail

nurse

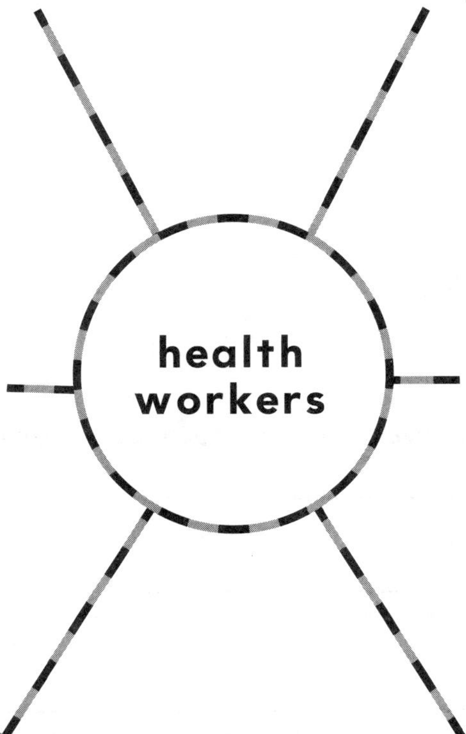

doctor

hospital

school

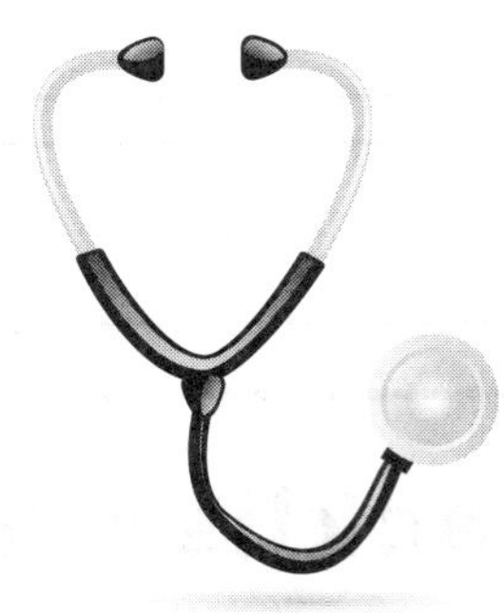

stethoscope

NAME: ______________________________

Directions: Read the text. Then, underline each sentence in green, red, or blue.

Green:	**Red:**	**Blue:**
topic	detail	closure

Health workers take care of people. A doctor works in a hospital. He uses a stethoscope. He helps people.

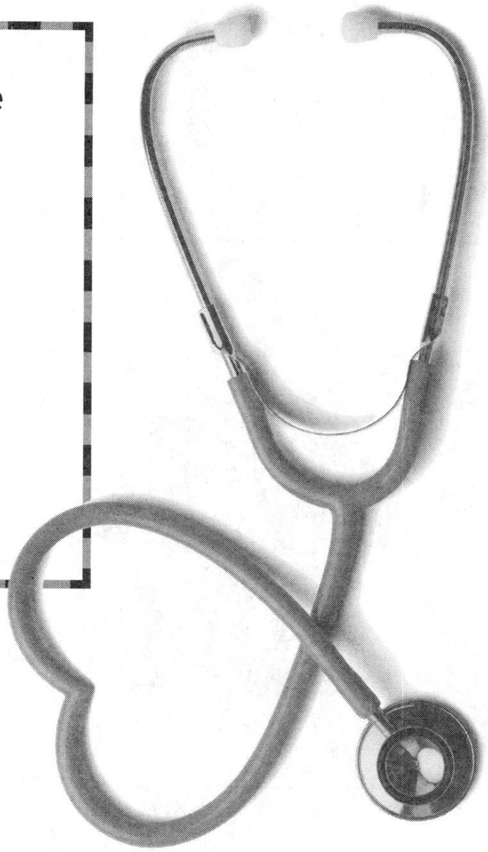

Printing Practice

Directions: Trace the word. Write it on your own.

doctor

NAME: ______________________________

Directions: Circle the correct pronoun for each person.

1.

he she

2.

he she

3.

he she

4.

he she

Boost Your Learning!

The pronoun *he* tells about boys or men.
The pronoun *she* tells about girls or women.

Example: Dad is a nurse. He is a nurse.

Mom is a doctor. She is a doctor.

NAME: ____________________

Directions: Practice writing each word two times.

1. of

2. uses

3. for

4. take

Boost Your Learning!

Some words do not follow spelling rules or patterns. You just have to learn to spell them!

Publishing
Health Workers

NAME: ______________________________

Directions: Read the text. Draw a picture to match. Then, fill in the checklist.

Health workers take care of people. A doctor works in a hospital. He uses a stethoscope. He helps people.

Checklist ☑

- ❑ Sentences begin with capital letters.
- ❑ Sentences end with punctuation.
- ❑ There are spaces between words.

NAME: ______________________________

Directions: Place check marks in the circles that have to do with safety helpers.

safety helpers

- cars
- firefighters
- police
- help people
- keep people safe
- brave
- pencils

NAME: ____________________

Directions: Use the Word Bank to help you write about safety helpers. Then, fill in the checklist.

Word Bank

officer help police fire

Safety helpers help people. A police __________ works at a __________ station. A firefighter works at a __________ station. These helpers __________ people.

Checklist ☑

- ❑ I have a topic sentence.
- ❑ I have a detail.
- ❑ I have a closing.

NAME: ______________________________

Directions: Write pronouns for the underlined words. Use the pictures to help you.

Pronouns

he she

1. *A* police officer stopped the car.

2. The firefighter used a hose.

Time to Improve!

Draw a safety helper. Write a pronoun to match.

Editing
Safety Helpers

NAME: ____________________

Directions: Write each word two times.

1. he

2. she

3. we

Time to Improve!

Directions: Read the sentence. Circle the word that is spelled incorrectly. Write the word correctly.

Seh went to help the people.

NAME: ______________________________

Directions: Draw and write about safety helpers. Then, fill in the checklist.

Checklist ☑

- ☐ Sentences begin with capital letters.
- ☐ Sentences end with punctuation.
- ☐ There are spaces between the words.

NAME: ______________________________

Directions: Circle the images that have parts of an apple in them.

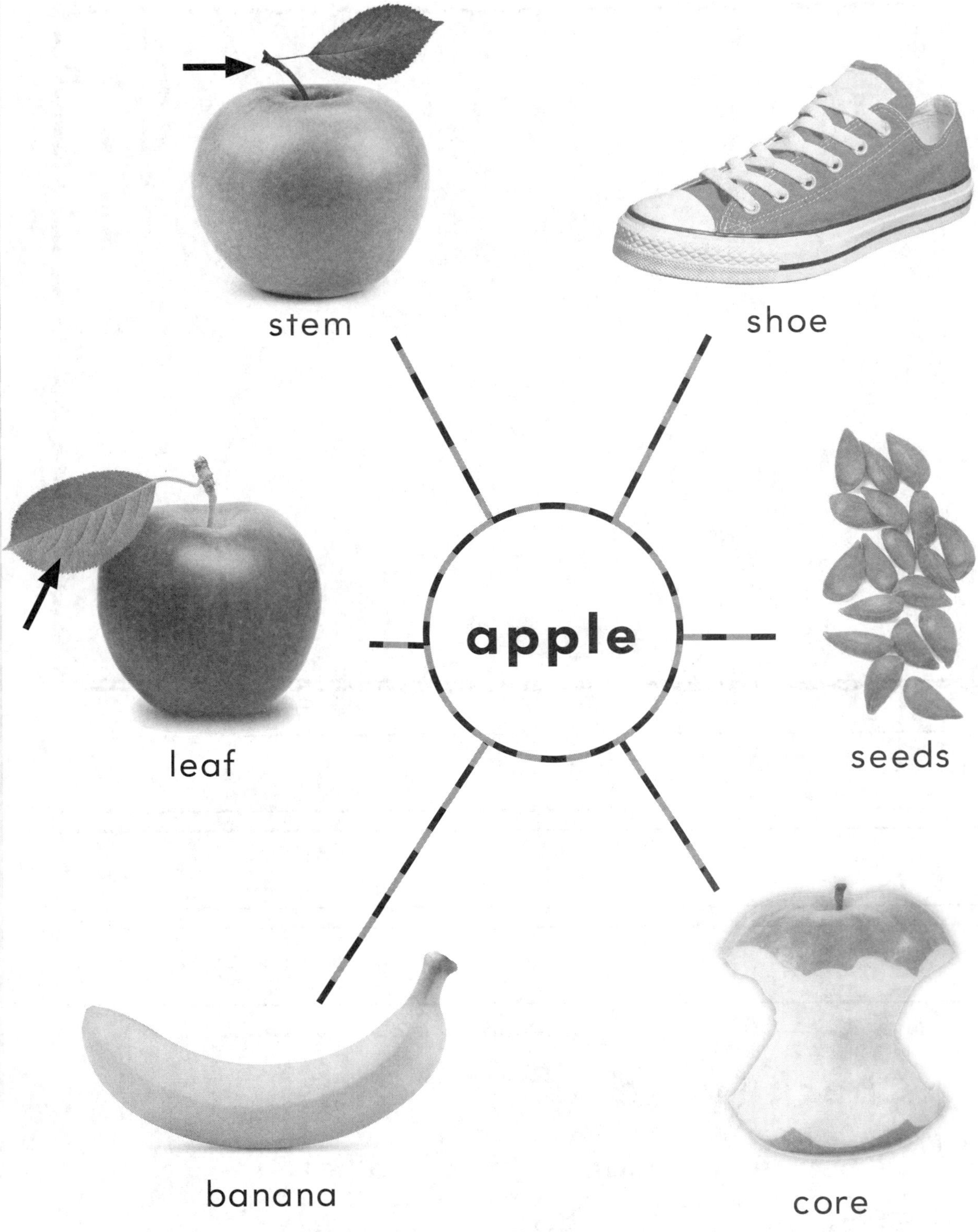

NAME: ______________________________

Directions: Read the text. Then, underline each sentence in green, red, or blue.

Green:	**Red:**	**Blue:**
topic	detail	closure

Fall is apple picking time! Apples grow on trees. Apples are red, green, and yellow. The middle of an apple is the core. It has the seeds. Do you like apples?

Printing Practice

abc

Directions: Trace the word. Write it on your own.

apple

NAME: ____________________

Revising
Apples

Directions: Two sentences are combined into one sentence. Circle the conjunctions **and** or **or**.

1. Apples can be red. Apples can be yellow.

   Apples can be red or yellow.

2. Apples have cores. Apples have seeds.

   Apple have cores and seeds.

3. Apples can be sweet. Apples can be sour.

   Apples can be sweet or sour.

4. Apples have stems. Apples have leaves.

   Apples have stems and leaves.

Boost Your Learning!

Sentences with the same ideas can be combined. Use the conjunctions **and** and **or** to combine them.

Example
Tam likes apple juice. Tam likes apple pie.

Tam likes apple juice **and** apple pie.

NAME: ______________________________

Directions: Read the apple jokes. Add question marks to the questions.

1. What kind of an apple isn't an apple ___?___   **Answer:** a pineapple
2. What lives in apples and loves to read ______   **Answer:** a bookworm
3. What did the apple say to the caterpillar ______   **Answer:** "Leaf me alone."
4. Why did the apple stop running ______   **Answer:** It ran out of juice.

Boost Your Learning!

Interrogative sentences need question marks as ending punctuation.

Publishing : Apples

NAME: ____________________

Directions: Read the text. Draw a picture to match. Then, fill in the checklist.

Fall is apple picking time! Apples grow on trees. Apples are red, green, and yellow. The middle is the core. It has the seeds. Do you like apples?

Checklist ☑

- ❑ Sentences begin with capital letters.
- ❑ Sentences end with punctuation.
- ❑ There are spaces between words.

NAME: ____

Directions: Circle the pictures that have parts of a pumpkin in them.

dog

rib

stem

pumpkin

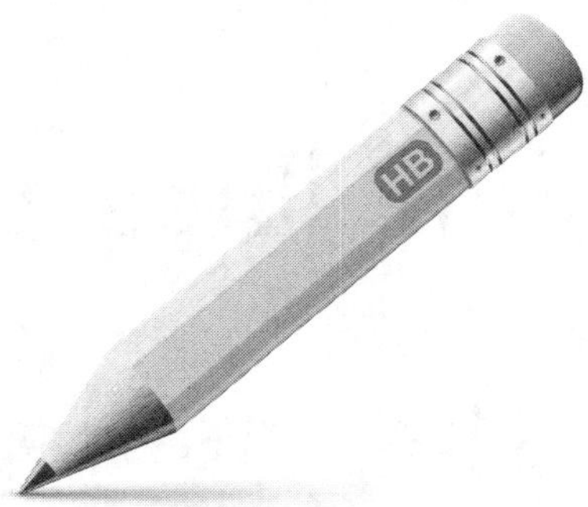

pencil

seeds

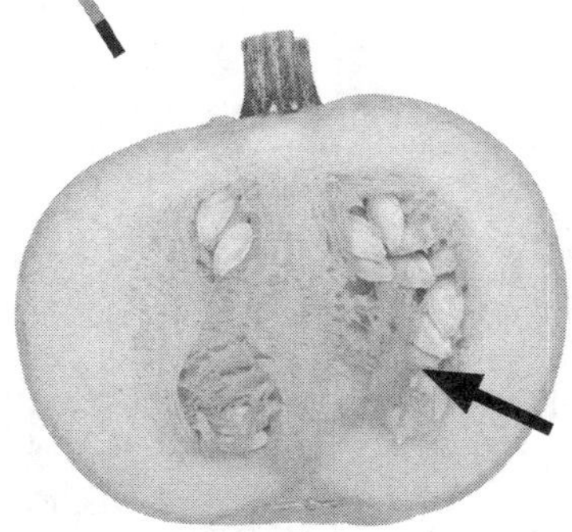

pulp

NAME: ______________________________

Directions: Use the Word Bank to help you write about a pumpkin. Then, fill in the checklist.

Word Bank

pumpkin seeds ribs pulp

Fall is ______________ picking time! Pumpkins are orange. The outside has lines called ______________. The inside has ______________ and ______________. Do you like pumpkins?

Checklist ☑

- ❑ I have a topic sentence.
- ❑ I have a detail.
- ❑ I have a closing.

NAME: ______________________________

Directions: Use the conjunctions **and** or **or** to combine the sentences into one sentence.

1. Pumpkins can be big. Pumpkins can be small.

Pumpkins can be big or small.

2. A pumpkin has pulp. A pumpkin has seeds. (*and*)

____

3. Pumpkins can be short. Pumpkins can be tall. (*or*)

____

NAME: ____________________

Directions: Add question marks to the questions. Then, draw lines to the correct answers.

Questions	**Answers**
1. What color is a pumpkin ?	fall
2. What are the lines on a pumpkin ___	orange
3. When are pumpkins picked ___	ribs
4. Where are the seeds ___	vine
5. What does a pumpkin grow on ___	inside

NAME: ________________________________

Directions: Draw and write about a pumpkin. Then, fill in the checklist.

Checklist ☑

- ☐ Sentences begin with capital letters.
- ☐ Sentences end with punctuation.
- ☐ There are spaces between the words.

NAME: ____

Directions: Read the opinion. Place check marks next to the reasons.

Opinion: Monsters are silly.

Reasons

_____ 1. They have claws.

_____ 2. They like to laugh.

_____ 3. They have crazy arms.

_____ 4. They have big noses.

_____ 5. They tell funny jokes.

NAME: ____________________

Directions: Read the text. Then, underline each sentence in green, red, or blue.

Green:	**Red:**	**Blue:**
opinion	detail	closure

I think monsters are silly. They have crazy arms. They tell funny jokes. I laugh when I see silly monsters.

Printing Practice

Directions: Trace the word. Write it on your own.

monster

NAME: ____________________

Directions: Write the words in order to show the word meanings.

Size Words

huge tiny little large

____
(**smallest**)

____

____

____
(**largest**)

Directions: Choose a word to complete the sentence.

This monster has a ____________________ nose.

NAME: ______________________________

Directions: Use the ≡ symbol to capitalize the months. Write them correctly on the lines.

1. Boo Boo's birthday is october 28.

   October

2. Popa's birthday is july 3.

   ____

3. december 23 is Ruffy's birthday.

   ____

4. Hip Hop's birthday is january 2.

   ____

Boost Your Learning!

Proper nouns need to be capitalized. The names of months are proper nouns.

NAME: ______________________________

Directions: Read the text. Draw a picture to match. Then, fill in the checklist.

I think monsters are silly. They have crazy arms. They tell funny jokes. I laugh when I see silly monsters.

Checklist ☑

- ❑ Sentences begin with capital letters.
- ❑ Sentences end with punctuation.
- ❑ There are spaces between words.

NAME: ______________________________

Directions: Draw a picture of your favorite candy. State your opinion. Then, write reasons why you like it.

Opinion

I like ______________________________.

Reasons

NAME: ____________________

Directions: Write about your favorite candy. Then, fill in the checklist.

Opinion

My favorite candy is ____________________

____________________.

Reasons

I like it because ____________________

____

____________________.

Closing Sentence

I love to eat ____________________.

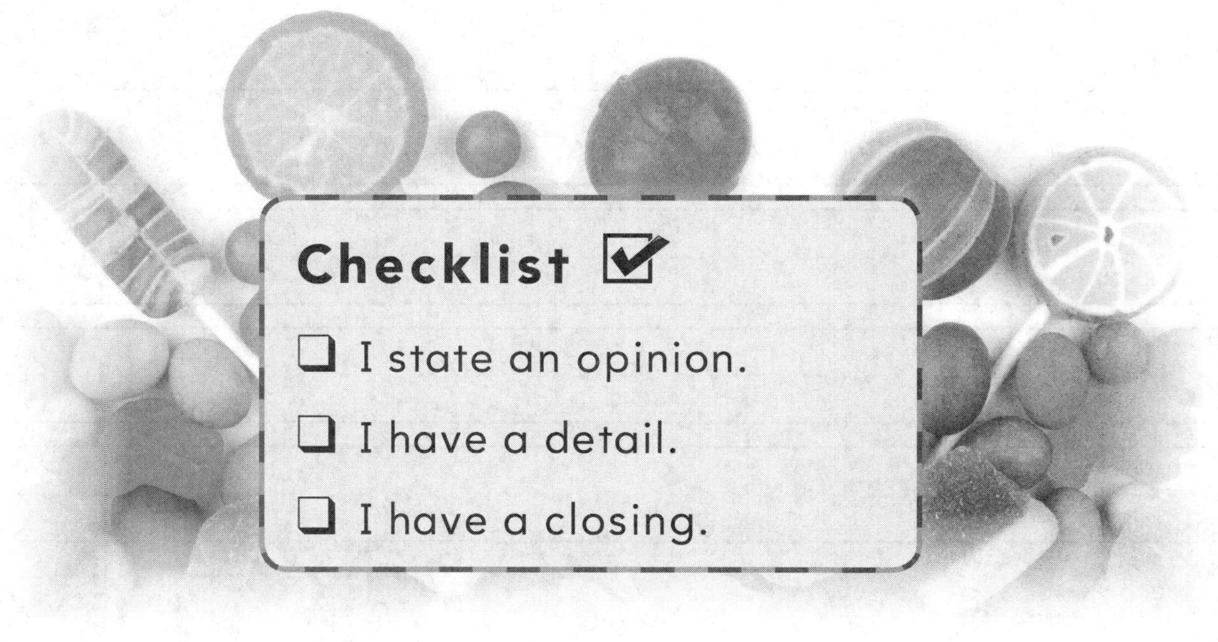

Checklist ☑

- ❑ I state an opinion.
- ❑ I have a detail.
- ❑ I have a closing.

NAME: ____________________

Directions: Write the Taste Words in order to show the word meanings.

Taste Words

delicious gross yummy disgusting

____

(**worst**)

____

____

____

(**best**)

Time to Improve!

Write a word about your favorite candy. Draw a picture.

____

NAME: ______________________________

Directions: Use the ≡ symbol to capitalize the months. Write the months correctly on the lines.

1. We carve pumpkins in october.

2. Thanksgiving is in november.

3. We give gifts in december.

Time to Improve!

Directions: Rewrite the sentence correctly.

My birthday is in november.

NAME: ______________________________

Directions: Draw and write about your favorite candy. Then, fill in the checklist.

Checklist ☑

- ☐ Sentences begin with capital letters.
- ☐ Sentences end with punctuation.
- ☐ There are spaces between the words.

NAME: ______________________________

Directions: Read the notes about a soccer game. Choose and underline one statement in each box.

Who?

my soccer team

my grandma

Where?

at the park

in my house

When?

at Christmas

at night

Event 1

I scored a goal.

I ate cookies.

Event 2

I went to camp.

I won the game.

NAME: ______________________________

Directions: Read the text. Then, underline each sentence in green, red, or blue.

Green:	**Red:**	**Blue:**
introduction	event	closure

My team had a soccer game at the park. When I got the ball, I aimed at the net. I kicked the winning goal. Everyone cheered for me. It was a great game!

Printing Practice

Directions: Trace the word. Write it on your own.

Soccer

NAME: ____

Directions: Read the text. Put an *X* next to each sentence below that adds more detail to the paragraph.

My team had a soccer game. I kicked the winning goal. Everyone cheered for me. My team won the game.

____ **1.** A soccer ball is round.

____ **2.** I aimed at the net.

____ **3.** My brother plays soccer, too.

____ **4.** We each got a trophy.

Remember!

Details should strengthen your writing by telling more about what happened.

NAME: ______________________________

Directions: Add exclamation points to the sentences.

1. I got a new soccer ball ____
2. My best friend is on my team ____
3. I scored a goal ____
4. We won the game ____
5. I got a trophy ____

Boost Your Learning!

Use **exclamation points** to show excitement.

Example: We won!

NAME: ______________________________

Directions: Read the text. Draw a picture to match. Then, fill in the checklist.

My team had a soccer game at the park. When I got the ball, I aimed at the net. I kicked the winning goal. Everyone cheered for me. It was a great game!

Checklist ☑

- ☐ Sentences begin with capital letters.
- ☐ Sentences end with punctuation.
- ☐ There are spaces between words.

NAME: ______________________________

Directions: Think about a basketball game. Complete the chart with notes about the game.

Who?

Where?

When?

Event 1 (Draw)	**Event 2** (Draw)

NAME: ____________________

Directions: Write about a basketball game. Then, fill in the checklist.

Introduction

I watched a basketball game with ____________________

____________________.

Events

First, ____________________.

____

Then, ____________________.

____

Closing Sentence

____

____________________ and I had so much fun!

Checklist ☑

- ☐ I have an introduction.
- ☐ I have two events.
- ☐ I have a closing.

NAME: ______________________________

Directions: Read each sentence. Circle the detail sentence that supports the original sentence.

1. I play on a basketball team.

   Detail 1: My team is called the Ravens.

   Detail 2: Our school has a basketball court.

2. We won our last game.

   Detail 1: Mark hurt his leg at the game.

   Detail 2: The score was 12 to 10.

3. The other team was ahead at half time.

   Detail 1: We played hard so we could win.

   Detail 2: The other team had seven people.

NAME: ______________________________

Directions: Read each sentence. Add a period (.) or an exclamation point (!) to the sentences.

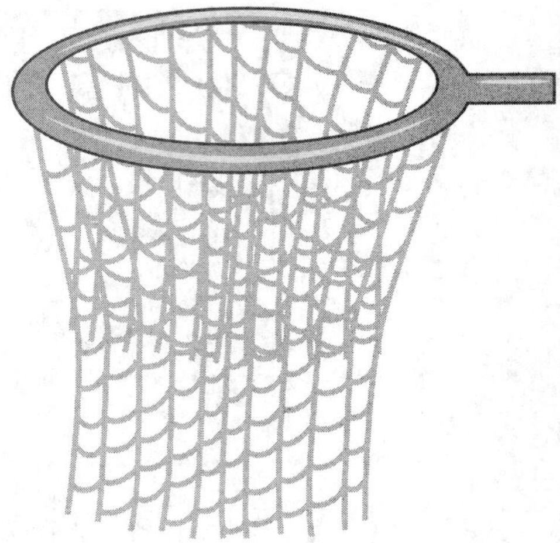

1. He scored ______
2. A basketball is orange ______
3. We are the champs ______
4. Throw the ball in the basket to score ______
5. She scored the winning basket ______

Time to Improve!

Directions: Write a sentence that needs an exclamation point as the ending mark.

____

____

NAME: ____________________

Directions: Draw and write about a basketball game. Then, fill in the checklist.

Checklist ☑

- ❑ Sentences begin with capital letters.
- ❑ Sentences end with punctuation.
- ❑ There are spaces between the words.

NAME: ______________________________

Directions: Read the text. Circle the pronouns.

Mom said the ducks fly south to stay warm. She told me the turtles buried themselves in the mud to hibernate. She said we will see the ducks and turtles again in the spring.

Boost Your Learning!

Pronouns take the place of nouns. They can make your writing more clear.

Example

Mom said we will see the ducks again in the spring.

Mom said we will see <u>them</u> again in the spring.

NAME: ______________________________

Directions: Draw a line to match the present tense verb with the past tense verb.

go	said
say	was
is	went
tell	saw
see	told

Boost Your Learning!

Use **past tense verbs** to show that events have already happened.

NAME: ____________________

Directions: Read the text. Draw a picture to match. Then, fill in the checklist.

It was winter. I went for a walk to the pond with my mom. I did not see any ducks or turtles. Mom said the ducks fly south to stay warm. She told me the turtles bury themselves in the mud to hibernate. We will see them again in the spring.

Checklist ☑

- ❑ Sentences begin with capital letters.
- ❑ Sentences end with punctuation.
- ❑ There are spaces between words.

NAME: ____

Directions: Think about dressing for winter weather. Complete the chart with notes about it.

Who? ______________________________

____

Where? ______________________________

When? ______________________________

Event 1 (Draw)	**Event 2** (Draw)

Editing

Dressing for the Weather

NAME: ____________________

Directions: Write the past tense verb from the Word Bank for each word.

Word Bank

wore	could	was	dressed

1. wear ____________________

2. is ____________________

3. can ____________________

4. dress ____________________

Time to Improve!

Directions: Rewrite the sentence correctly.

It is cold yesterday.

____

____

NAME: ____________________

Directions: Draw and write about dressing for a winter day. Then, fill in the checklist.

Checklist ☑

- ❑ Sentences begin with capital letters.
- ❑ Sentences end with punctuation.
- ❑ There are spaces between the words.

NAME: ______________________________

Directions: Read the opinion. Place check marks next to the reasons.

Opinion: It is fun to bake gingerbread men.

Reasons

_____ **1.** I get to decorate them.

_____ **2.** I get to eat them.

_____ **3.** They do not taste good.

_____ **4.** They are delicious.

_____ **5.** They make the house smell good.

NAME: ______________________________

Directions: Read the text. Then, underline each sentence in green, red, or blue.

Green:	**Red:**	**Blue:**
opinion	detail	closure

It is fun to bake gingerbread men. You get to decorate them. You also get to eat them. I look forward to baking gingerbread men in the winter.

Printing Practice abc

Directions: Trace the sentence.

Baking is fun!

Revising
Winter Traditions

NAME: ______________________________

Directions: Add a detail to each sentence. Use the questions to help you.

1. My favorite tradition is baking gingerbread men.

in winter

(**When is it done?**)

2. Decorating the cookies is fun to do.

(**What do you use for decorations?**)

3. I always look forward to baking gingerbread men.

(**Who do you do it with?**)

Boost Your Learning!

Adding more detail helps expand your sentence and makes it more interesting to read.

Example

Original Sentence: I love baking.

Expanded Sentence: I love baking with my mom.

NAME: ____

Directions: Add ending marks to the sentences.

Ending Marks

. ? !

1. Gingerbread men have raisin eyes
2. Baking with my mom is the best
3. There is a famous book about a gingerbread man
4. Do you love the smell of ginger
5. Gingerbread cookies are the best

Remember!

Declarative sentences end with periods.

Interrogative sentences end with question marks.

Exclamatory sentences end with exclamation points.

NAME: ____

Directions: Read the text. Draw a picture to match. Then, fill in the checklist.

It is fun to bake gingerbread men. You get to decorate them with raisins and candy. You also get to eat them. I look forward to baking gingerbread men in the winter.

Checklist ☑

- ☐ Sentences begin with capital letters.
- ☐ Sentences end with punctuation.
- ☐ There are spaces between words.

NAME: ______________________________

Directions: Draw your favorite winter celebration. State your opinion. Then, write reasons why you like it.

Opinion

I like ______________________________.

Reasons

____

____

____

____

NAME: ______________________________

Drafting

Winter Celebrations

Directions: Write about your favorite winter celebration. Then, fill in the checklist.

Opinion

My favorite winter celebration is ______________________________
______________________________.

Reasons

I like it because ______________________________
____
______________________________.

Closing Sentence

____
______________________________.

Checklist ☑

- ☐ I state an opinion.
- ☐ I have a detail.
- ☐ I have a closing.

NAME: ____________________

Directions: Look at the picture. Then, answer the questions with *where* and *who*.

1. Where can you hang lights?

   You can hang lights ____________________

2. Who can hang the lights?

   ____________________ can hang lights.

Time to Improve!

Directions: Write a detailed sentence about the picture above.

Detailed Sentence

____

____

NAME: ____________________________

Directions: Add ending marks to the sentences.

Ending Marks

. ? !

1. Do you know the seven principles of Kwanzaa

2. Hanukkah lasts seven days and eight nights

3. We got candy from the piñata at the Las Posadas celebration

4. Did you see the ice statues at the ice carnival

Time to Improve!

Directions: Rewrite the sentence correctly.

Where are the lights!

____

____

NAME: ________________________________

Directions: Draw and write about your favorite winter celebration. Then, fill in the checklist.

Checklist ☑

- ❑ Sentences begin with capital letters.
- ❑ Sentences end with punctuation.
- ❑ There are spaces between the words.

NAME: ______________________________

Directions: Read the opinion. Place check marks next to the reasons.

Opinion: It is fun to celebrate the new year!

Reasons

_____ **1.** I get to stay up late.

_____ **2.** I get to make lots of noise.

_____ **3.** I have to go to bed early.

_____ **4.** I get to throw confetti.

_____ **5.** It makes me cry.

NAME: ______________________________

Directions: Read the text. Then, underline each sentence in green, red, or blue.

Green:	**Red:**	**Blue:**
opinion	detail	closure

My favorite celebration is New Year's Eve. I get to stay up late. I get to throw confetti in the air. It is fun to ring in the new year.

Printing Practice

Directions: Trace the date. Write it on your own.

January 1

NAME: ______________________________

Revising · New Year

Directions: Rewrite each sentence with more detail.

1. I get to stay up late.

I get to stay up past my bedtime.

2. We blow horns.

3. People come to our house.

Boost Your Learning!

Add more detail to sentences by answering *how* or *why*.

Example
I get to stay up late.

I get to stay up until after midnight.

Editing
New Year

NAME: ______________________________

Directions: Read the sentences. One word is not correct. Circle it. Then, rewrite it on the line.

1. My favorite celebration iz New Year's Eve. ______ is

2. I get tu stay up late. ______

3. We toast to te new year. ______

4. Wee have noise makers. ______

5. It is fun to ring n the new year. ______

Publishing
New Year

NAME: ______________________________

Directions: Read the text. Draw a picture to match. Then, fill in the checklist.

My favorite celebration is New Year's Eve. I get to stay up late. I get to throw confetti in the air. It is fun to ring in the new year.

Checklist ☑

- ❑ Sentences begin with capital letters.
- ❑ Sentences end with punctuation.
- ❑ There are spaces between words.

NAME: ________________________________

Directions: Draw a picture of a Chinese New Year celebration. State your opinion. Then, write reasons why you like the celebration.

Word Bank

fun	dumplings	happy	fireworks
dragons	dancing	money	tea

Opinion

Chinese New Year is . . .

________________________________.

Reasons

____

____

____

NAME: ______________________

Directions: Write about a Chinese New Year celebration. Then, fill in the checklist.

Opinion

Celebrating Chinese New Year is ______________________.

Reasons

I like it because ______________________
______________________.

Closing Sentence

It is ______________ to celebrate Chinese New Year.

Checklist ☑

- ☐ I state an opinion.
- ☐ I have a detail.
- ☐ I have a closing.

NAME: ____________________________________

Directions: Use the words in the Word Bank to add details to the sentences.

Word Bank

get dragon yummy whole

1. A colorful ____________________ dances.

2. We ____________________ red envelopes.

3. My ____________________ family cleans.

4. We eat lots of ____________________ food.

Time to Improve!

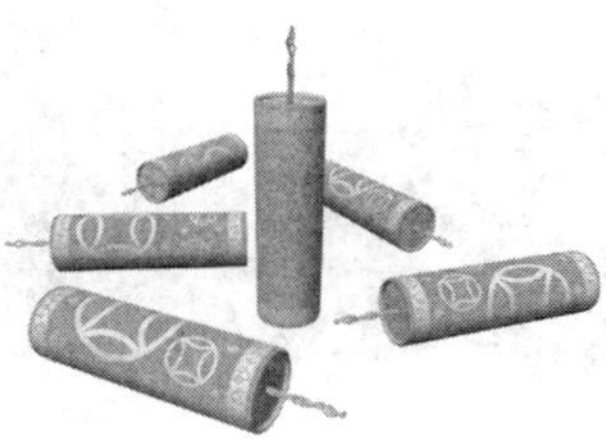

Directions: Circle the part of the sentence below that tells *how*.

We greet our friends **by bringing them food**.

NAME: ______________________________

Directions: Read each sentence. Circle the word that is not spelled correctly. Write the word correctly.

1. It iz a happy time. ____________

2. China haz over one billion people. ____________

3. The firecrackers r loud. ____________

4. Thay put flowers in their homes. ____________

5. Wee play games with the family. ____________

Time to Improve!

Directions: Write the commonly misspelled word twice.

they ____________ ____________

NAME: ____________________

Directions: Draw and write about a Chinese New Year celebration. Then, fill in the checklist.

Checklist ☑

- ☐ Sentences begin with capital letters.
- ☐ Sentences end with punctuation.
- ☐ There are spaces between the words.

NAME: ____________________

Directions: Read the opinion. Place check marks next to the reasons.

Opinion: Building a snowman is great!

Reasons

____ 1. I get to make a face.

____ 2. I get to play with snow.

____ 3. It falls apart.

____ 4. I watch the snowman while I sip hot cocoa.

____ 5. I give my snowman a name.

NAME: ____________________

Directions: Read the text. Then, underline each sentence in green, red, or blue.

Green:	**Red:**	**Blue:**
opinion	detail	closure

Making a snowman is great! I get to play with snow. I get to name my snowman. I watch my snowman while I drink hot cocoa. It is fun to build a snowman.

Printing Practice

Directions: Trace the sentence.

I like snowmen.

NAME: ______________________________

Directions: Sort the words into the correct rows.

Transition Words

First	Finally	Then
Next	To begin	Lastly

Beginning Sentence

Middle Sentence

Ending Sentence

Boost Your Learning!

Transition words help guide the reader through the paragraph. They tell the reader something is going to change.

Example: First, I will eat breakfast. Then, I will go to school.

NAME: ______________________________

Directions: Add commas to the sentences.

1. Roll big, medium, and small snowballs.

2. Put on a carrot nose button eyes and a coal mouth.

3. Add a scarf a hat and stick arms.

4. A snowman can be a boy a girl or a baby.

Boost Your Learning!

Use **commas** to separate items in a list.

NAME: ______________________________

Directions: Read the text. Draw a picture to match. Then, fill in the checklist.

Making a snowman is great! I get to play with snow. I get to name my snowman. I watch my snowman while I drink hot cocoa. It is fun to build a snowman.

Checklist ☑

- ❑ Sentences begin with capital letters.
- ❑ Sentences end with punctuation.
- ❑ There are spaces between words.

NAME: ____________________

Directions: Draw a picture of your favorite winter sport. State your opinion. Then, write reasons why you like it.

Opinion

I like ____________________.

Reasons

NAME: ______________________________

Directions: Write about your favorite winter sport. Then, fill in the checklist.

Opinion

My favorite winter sport is ______________________________.

Reasons

I like it because ______________________________
______________________________.

Closing Sentence

I love playing ______________________________.

Checklist ☑

- ❑ I state an opinion.
- ❑ I have a detail.
- ❑ I have a closing.

NAME: ______________________________

Directions: Write transition words in the blanks to help show order.

Transition Words

First	Finally	Then	Next
To begin	Third	Lastly	Second

Beginning Sentence

______________________, I carry the sled up the hill.

Middle Sentence

______________________, I sit down on the sled.

Ending Sentence

______________________, I slide down the hill.

Time to Improve!

Complete the sentence with a word from above.

______________________, I carry the sled up the hill.

NAME: ______________________________

Directions: Add commas to the sentences.

1. I like to sled ski and skate.
2. It is fun to watch hockey snowboarding and skiing.
3. You need skis poles and boots to ski.

Time to Improve!

Directions: Read the sentences. Combine them into one sentence. Add two commas.

Winter has ice. Winter has wind. Winter has snow.

NAME: ______________________________

Directions: Draw and write about your favorite winter sport. Then, fill in the checklist.

Checklist ☑

- ❑ Sentences begin with capital letters.
- ❑ Sentences end with punctuation.
- ❑ There are spaces between the words.

NAME: ____

Directions: Place check marks in the circles that have to do with Dr. Martin Luther King Jr.

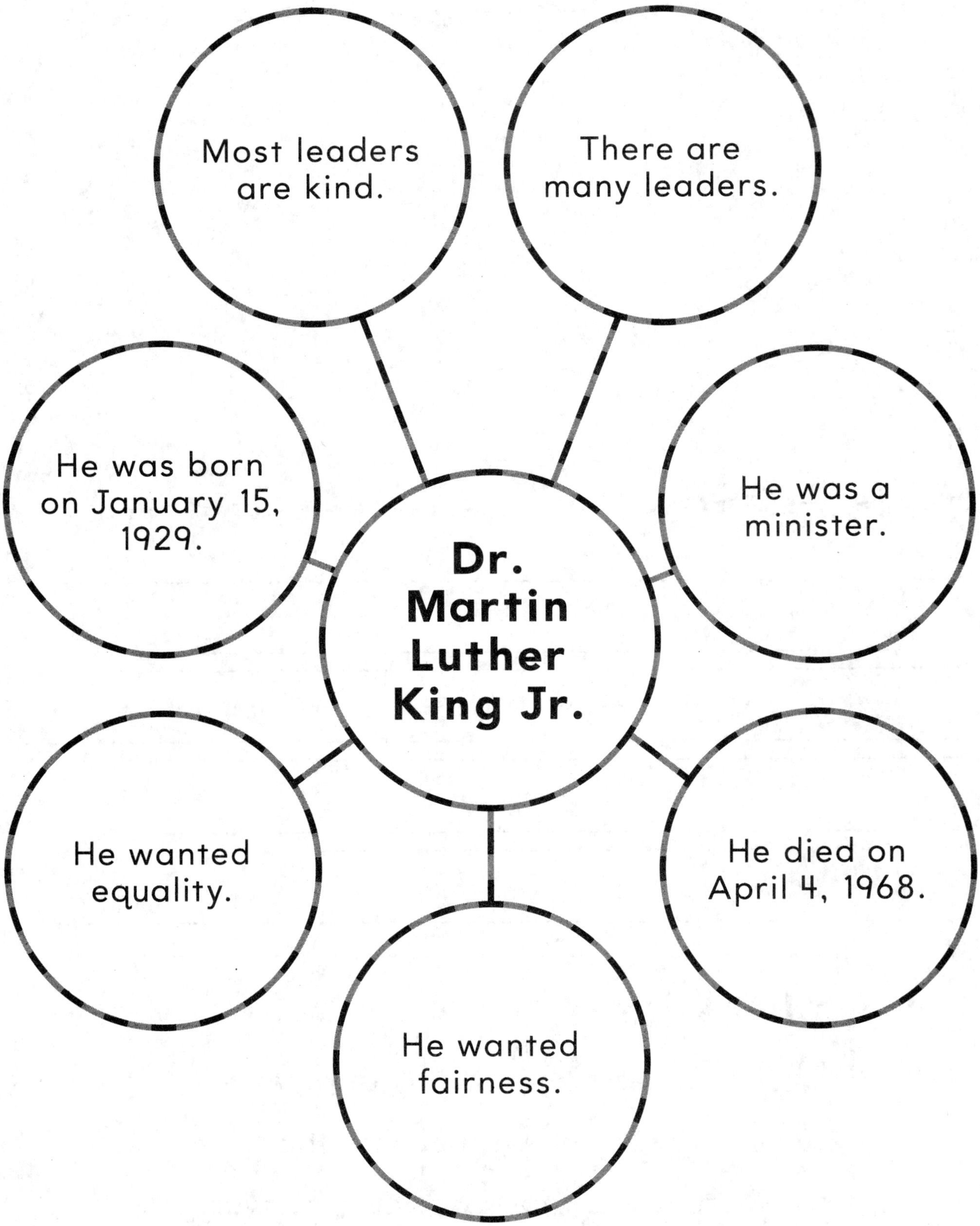

NAME: ______________________________________

Directions: Read the text. Then, underline each sentence in green, red, or blue.

Green:	**Red:**	**Blue:**
topic	detail	closure

Martin Luther King Jr. was an important leader. He planned boycotts. He gave speeches. He was a great man.

Printing Practice abc

Directions: Trace the sentence.

King was a leader.

NAME: ______________________________

Directions: Circle the first word in each sentence. Rewrite the sentences so they start with the pronoun **he**.

1. King married in 1953.

2. King planned boycotts.

3. King gave speeches.

Boost Your Learning!

The same thing can be said in different ways. Change the first word in a sentence to make it more clear.

Example
Martin was a minister.

He was a minister.

NAME: ____________________________________

Directions: Read the sentences. Use the ≡ symbol to show the names that need to be capitalized.

1. michael king was born in 1929.
2. His name was changed to martin in 1934.
3. King's sister was named willie.
4. His brother was named alfred.

Remember!

Names of people are proper nouns. They need to begin with capital letters.

martin luther king jr. Martin Luther King Jr.

NAME: ____________________

Directions: Read the text. Draw a picture to match. Then, fill in the checklist.

Martin Luther King Jr. was an important leader. He planned boycotts. He gave speeches. He was a great man.

Checklist ☑

- ❑ Sentences begin with capital letters.
- ❑ Sentences end with punctuation.
- ❑ There are spaces between words.

NAME: ______________________________

Directions: Place check marks next to the circles that have to do with George Washington.

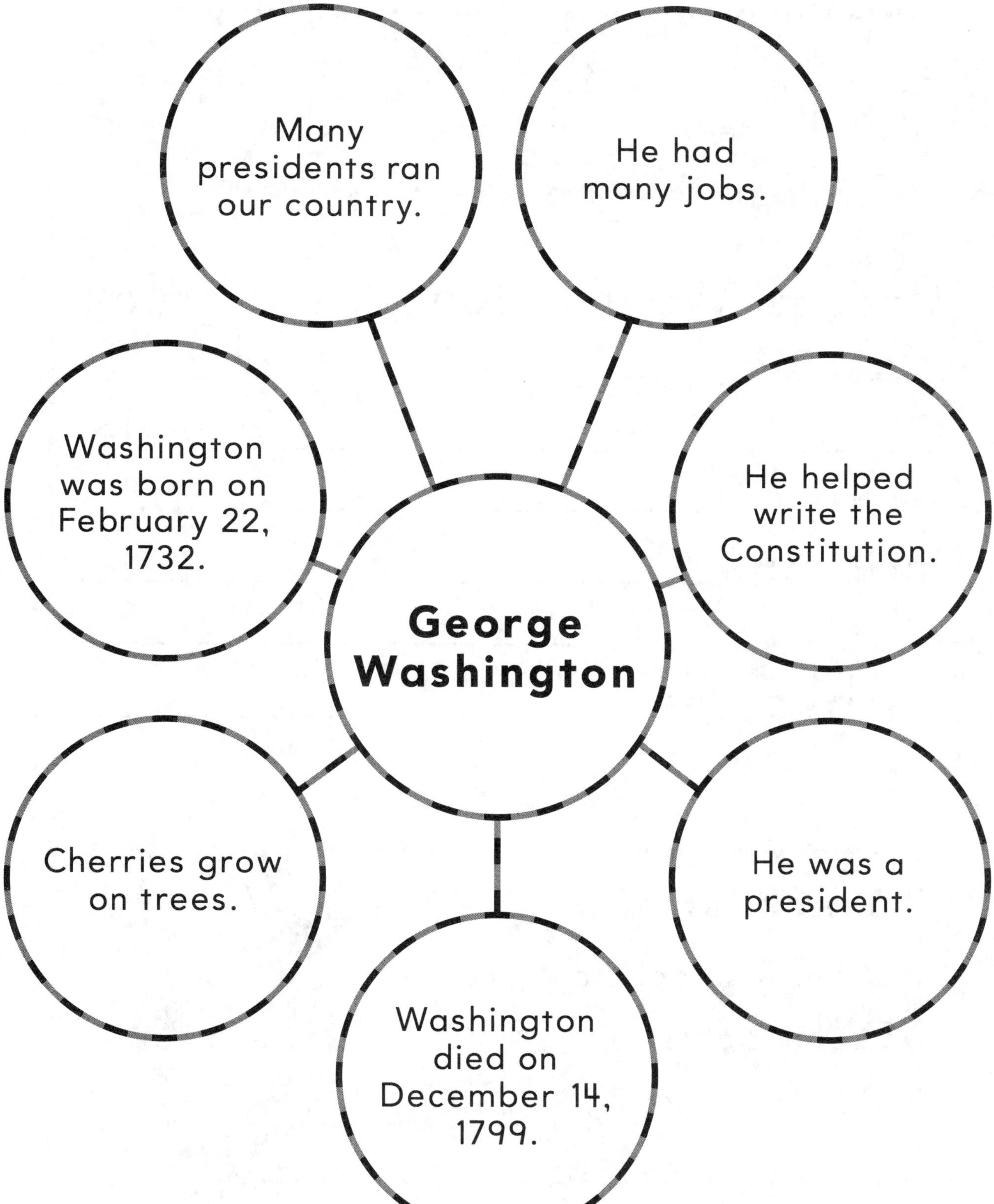

NAME: ______________________

Directions: Use the Word Bank to help you write about George Washington. Then, fill in the checklist.

Word Bank

leader president army

George Washington was a great

______________________. He

lead an ______________________.

He became ______________________.

Checklist ☑

- ❑ I have a topic sentence.
- ❑ I have a detail.
- ❑ I have a closing.

NAME: ______________________________

Directions: Circle the first word in each sentence. Complete the sentences with **he** or **his**.

1. Washington was born in 1732.

   ____________ was born in 1732.

2. Washington's home was Mount Vernon.

   ____________ home was Mount Vernon.

3. Washington married Martha Custis.

   ____________ married Martha Custis.

4. Washington's job was president.

   ____________ job was president.

Time to Improve!

Directions: Complete the sentence with a pronoun.

Washington was a great leader.

____________________ was a great leader.

NAME: ____

Directions: Read the notes about your family. Choose and underline one statement in each box.

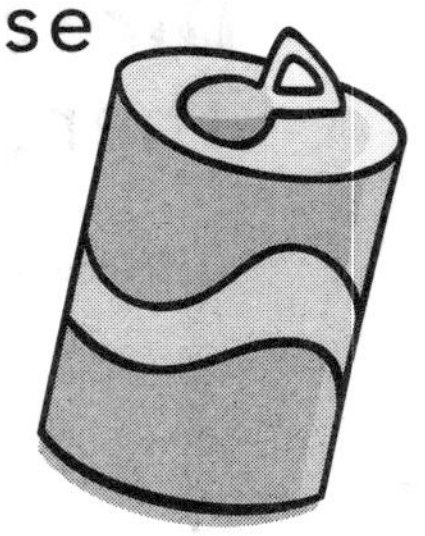

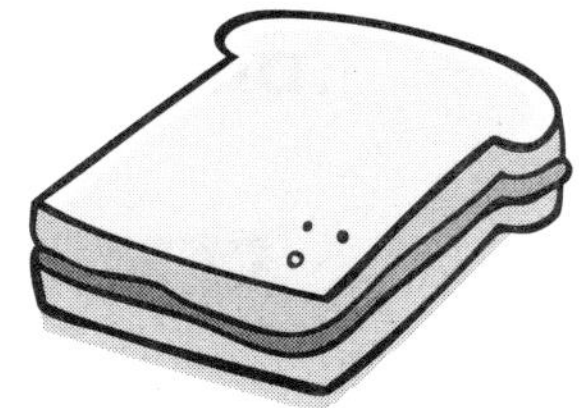

Who?

my family

my friends

Where?

at the park

in my classroom

When?

late at night

during the day

Event 1

We packed lunches.

I went to school.

Event 2

I went to a friend's house.

We went on a picnic.

NAME: ______________________________

Directions: Read the text. Then, underline each sentence in green, red, or blue.

Green:	**Red:**	**Blue:**
introduction	event	closure

One time, I went on a picnic with my family. First, my mom packed a picnic lunch in a basket. Then, we went to Duck Park. It was fun to spend time with my family.

Printing Practice

Directions: Trace the sentence.

I love my family.

Revising
Family

NAME: ______________________________

Directions: Write transition words on the lines below.

Beginning	Middle	End
Once One time	First Then	Finally Lastly

______________________, I went on a picnic.

______________________, my mom packed a lunch.

______________________, we went to Duck Park.

______________________, we went home.

Boost Your Learning!

Transition words help show the order events happen in.

Example
First, I hugged my mom. Then, I hugged my dad.

NAME: ____________________

Directions: Read the paragraph. Use the Editing Marks to add periods and capitalize the correct letters.

Editing Marks

⨀ ≡

My family went for a bike ride. first, we got ready to go Then, we rode to the park. when we got to the park, we fed the ducks We had a lot of fun.

Remember!

A sentence begins with a capital letter.
A sentence has to have an ending mark.

NAME: ______________________________

Directions: Write about playing with a friend. Then, fill in the checklist.

I played with ______________________________.

First, we ______________________________

____.

Then, we ______________________________

____.

______________________________ and I had so much fun!

Checklist ☑

- ❑ I have an introduction.
- ❑ I have two events.
- ❑ I have a closing.

NAME: ____________________

Directions: Complete the sentences about something fun you have done with a friend. Use the transition words to help you.

____

First, ____________________

____

____

Then, ____________________

____

Time to Improve!

Directions: Write two transition words that will work for the sentence.

____________, I went to the zoo with my friend.

____________, I went to the zoo with my friend.

Editing · Friends

NAME: ____

Directions: Edit the text below. Use the Editing Marks to add periods and capitalize letters correctly.

Editing Marks

⊙ ≡

I had a play date with my friend, Max First, we played with my toy cars. next, we dug holes in the backyard. we had a great time together

Time to Improve!

Directions: Complete the sentence.

A sentence ______________________ with a period.
(**ends** or **begins**)

NAME: ______________________________

Directions: Draw and write about playing with a friend. Then, fill in the checklist.

Checklist ☑

- ❑ Sentences begin with capital letters.
- ❑ Sentences end with punctuation.
- ❑ There are spaces between the words.

Prewriting Pie

NAME: ______________________________

Directions: Read the opinion. Place check marks next to the reasons.

Opinion: Apple pie is delicious!

Reasons

_____ **1.** It has a flaky crust.

_____ **2.** They like to laugh.

_____ **3.** It is sweet.

_____ **4.** It tastes good warm.

_____ **5.** It has fresh apples from a tree.

NAME: ______________________________

Directions: Read the text. Then, underline each sentence in green, red, or blue.

Green:	**Red:**	**Blue:**
opinion	detail	closure

Apple pie is delicious. It has a yummy crust. It has crisp, fresh apples in it. I always have room for apple pie!

Printing Practice abc

Directions: Trace the sentence.

I love apple pie.

Revising: Pie

NAME: ____________________

Directions: Read the topic sentences. Write new words for the underlined words.

1. In my opinion, apple pie is the best.

2. I love apple pie.

3. I like to eat apple pie.

Boost Your Learning!

Try to make a topic sentence interesting to make the reader want to read more!

Example: If I could have any pie, it would be apple pie!

Editing

Pie

NAME: ____________________

Directions: Follow the spelling pattern. Write the words for each picture.

bake

1. 

2. 

3. 

Remember!

Words that rhyme are often spelled the same. Use the spelling patterns of words you know to help you spell words you do not know.

NAME: ______________________________

Directions: Read the text. Draw a picture to match. Then, fill in the checklist.

Apple pie is delicious. It has a yummy crust. It has crisp, fresh apples in it. I always have room for apple pie!

Checklist ☑

- ❑ Sentences begin with capital letters.
- ❑ Sentences end with punctuation.
- ❑ There are spaces between words.

NAME: ______________________________

Directions: Draw a picture of your favorite pizza. State your opinion. Then, write reasons why you like it.

Opinion

I like ______________________________.

Reasons

____

____

____

____

Drafting

Pizza

NAME: ____________________

Directions: Write about your favorite kind of pizza. Then, fill in the checklist.

My favorite pizza is ____________________

____________________. I like it

because ____________________

____________________.

I love to eat ____________________.

Checklist ☑

- ❑ I state an opinion.
- ❑ I have a detail.
- ❑ I have a closing.

NAME: ____________________

Directions: Write your favorite kind of pizza on the lines. Then, finish the opinion below with the number of your favorite topic sentence.

1. In my opinion, ____________________ is the best kind of pizza.

2. I love ____________________ pizza.

3. I like to eat ____________________ pizza.

4. I think ____________________ pizza is the best.

My favorite topic sentence is number ______.

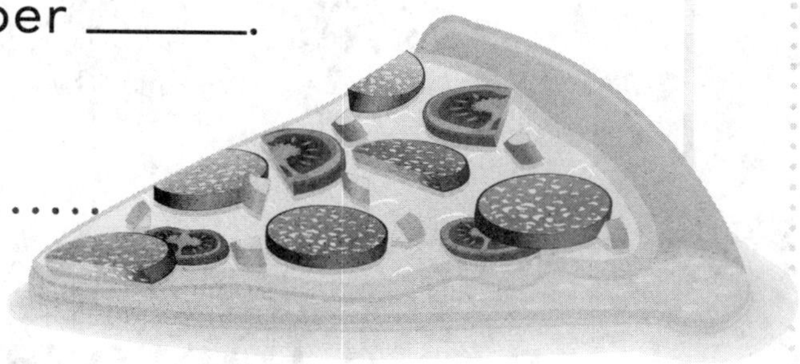

Time to Improve!

Directions: Add details the topic sentence below.

I love cold pizza.

____

____

NAME: ______________________

Directions: Follow the spelling pattern. Write the words for each picture.

slice

1. 

2. 

3. 

Time to Improve!

Directions: Read the sentence. Circle the words that are spelled incorrectly. Write the words correctly.

I liek to eat pzza.

NAME: ______________________________

Directions: Draw and write about your favorite pizza. Then, fill in the checklist.

Checklist ☑

- ☐ Sentences begin with capital letters.
- ☐ Sentences end with punctuation.
- ☐ There are spaces between the words.

Prewriting
Airplanes

NAME: ____________________

Directions: Read the notes about going on a plane. Choose and underline one statement in each box.

Who?

my grandparents

my classmates

Where?

on a plane

in my house

When?

during school

during the day

Event 1

We boarded the plane.

We went to the park.

Event 2

We went to sleep.

We flew to New York.

NAME: ______________________________

Directions: Read the text. Then, underline each sentence in green, red, or blue.

Green:	**Red:**	**Blue:**
introduction	event	closure

My grandparents and I went on a trip. First, we packed our bags. Then, we drove to the airport. Next, we flew on a plane. We landed safely in New York. We had a wonderful trip.

Printing Practice abc

Directions: Trace the sentence.

Planes fly high.

NAME: ______________________________

Directions: Draw lines through two sentences that do not support the introduction sentence.

Introduction Sentence

I went on an airplane for the first time last summer.

1. We drove to the airport.
2. My dad drives a pick-up truck.
3. We flew to New York.
4. My grandpa picked us up from the airport.
5. My grandpa has gray hair.

Boost Your Learning!

Every sentence should support the topic of the paragraph.

NAME: ______________________________

Directions: Write the article **a** or **an** in front of each noun.

1.

______ airplane

2.

______ grandpa

3.

______ truck

4.

______ airport

Boost Your Learning!

Use **a** if the next word begins with a consonant. (**a bag**)

Use **an** if the next word begins with a vowel. (**an ant**)

NAME: ______________________________

Directions: Read the text. Draw a picture to match. Then, fill in the checklist.

My grandparents and I went on a trip. First, we packed our bags. Then, we drove to the airport. Then, we flew on a plane. Finally, we landed safely in New York. We had a wonderful trip.

Checklist ☑

- ☐ Sentences begin with capital letters.
- ☐ Sentences end with punctuation.
- ☐ There are spaces between words.

NAME: ______________________________

Directions: Think about flying a kite. Complete the chart with notes about it.

Who? ______________________________

____

Where? ______________________________

When? ______________________________

Event 1 (Draw)	**Event 2** (Draw)

NAME: ____________________

Directions: Write about flying a kite. Then, fill in the checklist.

____________________ and I flew kites.

First, ____________________
____________________.

Then, ____________________
____________________.

____________________ and I had so much fun!

Checklist ☑

- ❑ I have an introduction.
- ❑ I have two events.
- ❑ I have a closing.

NAME: ______________________________

Directions: Draw lines through two sentences that do not support the introduction sentence.

Introduction Sentence

I saw a man flying a kite.

1. The man had a beard.
2. The kite was the shape of a whale.
3. I watched the man make the kite do tricks.
4. The ocean water was cold that day.
5. He let me fly the kite.

Time to Improve!

Directions: Explain why the sentences you crossed out do not support the topic sentence.

NAME: ______________________________

Directions: Read each sentence. Write **a** or **an** on each blank.

1. I went to the beach and saw ______ man flying ______ kite.

2. The kite was the shape of ______ whale.

3. There was ______ ribbon tied on the kite string.

4. He made the kite do ______ exciting trick.

5. He said he had ______ eel-shaped kite, too.

Time to Improve!

Directions: Write a noun after each article. Pay attention to the letter the noun begins with.

a ______________________

an ______________________

NAME: ______________________________

Directions: Draw and write about flying a kite. Then, fill in the checklist.

Checklist ☑

- ☐ Sentences begin with capital letters.
- ☐ Sentences end with punctuation.
- ☐ There are spaces between the words.

NAME: ____

Directions: Circle the pictures that have to do with hens.

NAME: ______________________________

Directions: Read the text. Then, underline each sentence in green, red, or blue.

Green:	**Red:**	**Blue:**
topic	detail	closure

The life cycle of a hen is neat. The mother hen lays an egg. She sits on the egg to keep it warm. The baby chick pecks its way out of the egg. It grows up to be a hen. The life cycle starts again when the hen lays an egg.

Printing Practice abc

Directions: Trace the sentence.

Baby chicks are cute!

NAME: ______________________________

Directions: The paragraph is out of order. Use numbers to show the correct order. Read the sentences again in order.

Introduction The life cycle of a hen is neat.

☐ The baby chick pecks its way out of the egg.

☐ The mother hen sits on the egg to keep it warm.

☐ The mother hen lays an egg.

☐ The baby chick grows up to be a hen.

Conclusion The life cycle starts again when the hen lays an egg.

NAME: ____________________

Directions: Circle the singular noun in each sentence. Underline the singular verb.

1. The mother hen lays an egg.
2. She sits on the egg.
3. The baby chick pecks its way out of the egg.
4. It grows up to be a hen.

Boost Your Learning!

Make sure the nouns and verbs match when writing sentences.

- **Singular nouns** need singular verbs to match.
- **Plural nouns** need plural verbs to match.

NAME: ______________________________

Directions: Read the text. Draw a picture to match. Then, fill in the checklist.

The life cycle of a hen is neat. The mother hen lays an egg. She sits on the egg to keep it warm. The baby chick pecks its way out of the egg. It grows up to be a hen. The life cycle starts again when the hen lays an egg.

Checklist ☑

- ❑ Sentences begin with capital letters.
- ❑ Sentences end with punctuation.
- ❑ There are spaces between words.

NAME: ______________________________

Directions: Circle the pictures that have to do with plants.

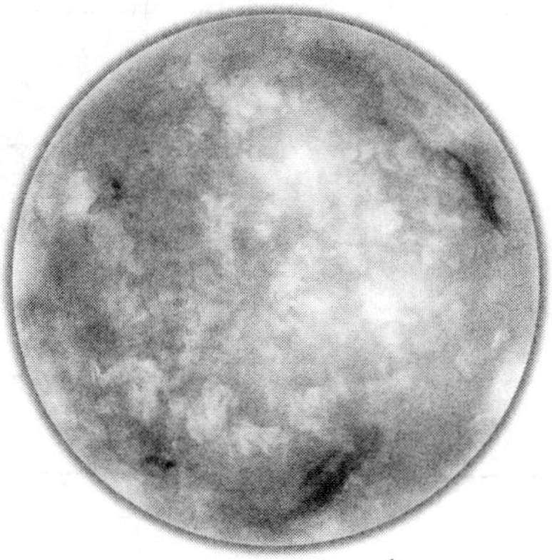
sun

baby chick

plants

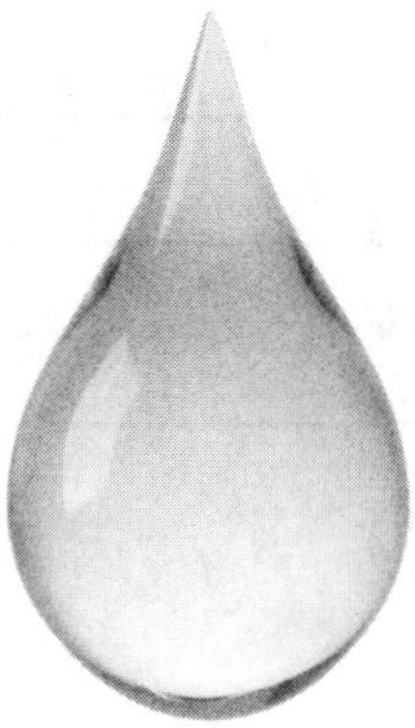
water

leaves

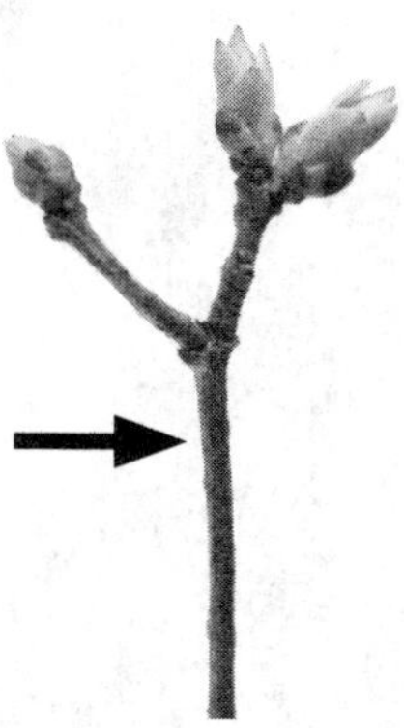
stem

skateboard

NAME: ______________________________

Drafting
Plants

Directions: Write about plants. Then, fill in the checklist.

Plants are ______________________.

They have ______________________

____

______________________________________.

Plants are ______________________.

Checklist ☑

- ❑ I have a topic sentence.
- ❑ I have a detail.
- ❑ I have a closing.

NAME: ______________________________

Directions: Write pronouns for the underlined words.

Word Bank

She It He

1. Tom likes plants.

____

2. Mrs. Jones grows many plants.

____

3. The plant grows tall.

____

Time to Improve!

Directions: Write a pronoun that can be used for each word.

plant ______________________________

plants ______________________________

NAME: ____________________

Directions: Complete each sentence with the correct verb.

Singular
A plant

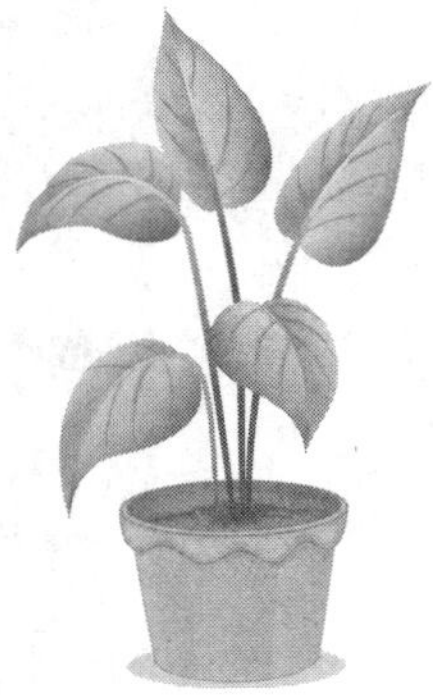

Plural
Plants

Verb Choices		Sentences
Singular	**Plural**	
has	have	Plants ____________ leaves.
needs	need	A plant ____________ water.
grows	grow	Plants ____________ in soil.

Time to Improve!

Directions: Circle the incorrect verb in the sentence. Write the verb correctly on the line below.

Plants grows flowers.

____

NAME: ______________________________

Directions: Draw a and write about a plant. Then, fill in the checklist.

Checklist ☑

- ❑ Sentences begin with capital letters.
- ❑ Sentences end with punctuation.
- ❑ There are spaces between the words.

Prewriting
Transportation

NAME: ______________________________

Directions: Read the notes about a boat ride. Choose and underline one statement in each box.

Who?

my teacher

my family

Where?

on the ocean

on land

When?

on vacation

at night

Event 1

We packed our bags.

We watched a movie.

Event 2

We sailed to the Bahamas.

We flew on a plane.

NAME: ______________________________

Directions: Read the text. Then, underline each sentence in green, red, or blue.

Green:	**Red:**	**Blue:**
introduction	event	closure

Last summer, my family went on vacation. We went on a boat. First, we packed our bags. Then, we drove to the boat. After we boarded, we sailed for three days. It was a really fun trip!

Printing Practice abc

Directions: Trace the sentence.

I like to travel.

NAME: ____________________

Directions: Read the two sentences. Read the combined sentence. Circle the conjunction. The first one is done for you.

1. We flew for three hours. Then, we were there.

   We flew for three hours, and then we were there.

2. She could travel by car. She could travel by train.

   She could travel by car or train.

3. It was fun flying. It was fun getting there so fast.

   It was fun flying and getting there so fast.

Remember!

Conjunctions are words that connect sentences. Some conjunctions are: **and**, **but**, **or**, **so**, and **because**.

NAME: ____________________

Directions: Circle the past tense verbs in the paragraph.

This summer I went on an airplane. My family took a trip to see my great-grandma. We flew for three hours. My grandma picked us up at the airport. It was fun flying and getting there so fast.

Directions: Write the past tense of each verb.

1. pick ____________________
2. make ____________________
3. go ____________________
4. is ____________________

Publishing
Transportation

NAME: ____________________________________

Directions: Read the text. Draw a picture to match. Then, fill in the checklist.

Last summer, my family went on vacation. We went on a boat. First, we packed our bags. Then, we drove to the boat. After we boarded, we sailed for three days. It was a really fun trip!

Checklist ☑

- ☐ Sentences begin with capital letters.
- ☐ Sentences end with punctuation.
- ☐ There are spaces between words.

NAME: ____________________

Directions: Think about technology. Complete the chart with notes about using it.

Who?

Where?

When?

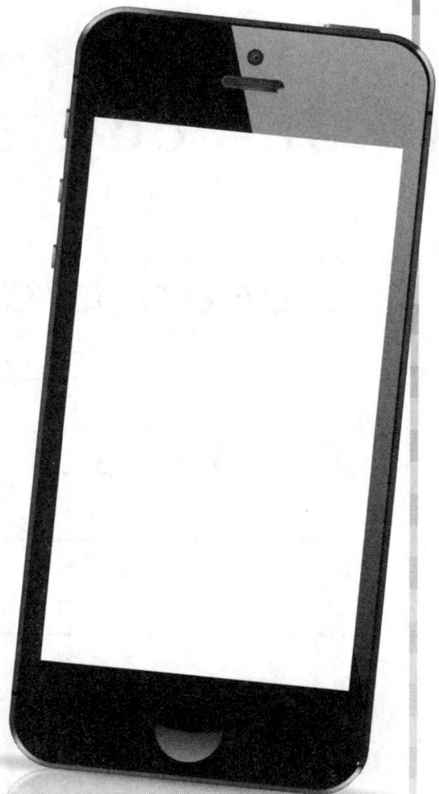

Event 1 (Draw)	**Event 2** (Draw)

NAME: ______________________________

Drafting
Technology

Directions: Write about technology. Then, fill in the checklist.

One day, ______________________________ and

I used a/an ______________________________.

First, ______________________________.

______________________________.

Then, ______________________________.

______________________________.

______________________________ and I had so much fun!

Checklist ☑

- ❑ I have an introduction.
- ❑ I have two events.
- ❑ I have a closing.

NAME: ______________________________

Directions: Circle each conjunction used to combine the two sentences.

1. You can type on a typewriter. You can type on a computer.

You can type on a typewriter and on a computer.

2. Dial phones had cords. You had to stay close to the phone.

Dial phones had cords, so you had to stay close to the phone.

3. You used to have to get up to change the channel on TV. There was not a remote control.

You used to have to get up to change the channel on TV because there was not a remote control.

Time to Improve!

Directions: Complete the sentence with a conjunction.

My mom played outside when she was little,

____

______________________ there were no video games.

NAME: ______________________________

Editing

Technology

Directions: Circle the past tense verbs in the paragraph.

My mom and I walked by a store. I saw something strange in the window. I didn't know what it was. My mom said it was a typewriter. She said that when she went to school that is what she typed on. I thought it was funny because I use a computer.

Time to Improve!

Directions: Write this sentence using a past tense verb.

I go to school today.

____

____

NAME: ______________________________

Directions: Draw and write about technology. Then, fill in the checklist.

Checklist ☑

- ❑ Sentences begin with capital letters.
- ❑ Sentences end with punctuation.
- ❑ There are spaces between the words.

NAME: ______________________________

Directions: Place check marks in the circles that have to do with butterflies.

butterflies

- They have wings.
- There are many insects in the world.
- Butterflies are insects.
- They lay eggs.
- They begin as caterpillars.
- They fly.
- Animals can crawl.

NAME: ______________________________

Directions: Read the text. Then, underline each sentence in green, red, or blue.

Green:	**Red:**	**Blue:**
topic	detail	closure

Butterflies are a type of insect. They have wings that let them fly. Their wings have patterns. They fly to flowers. They sip the nectar. Butterflies are interesting!

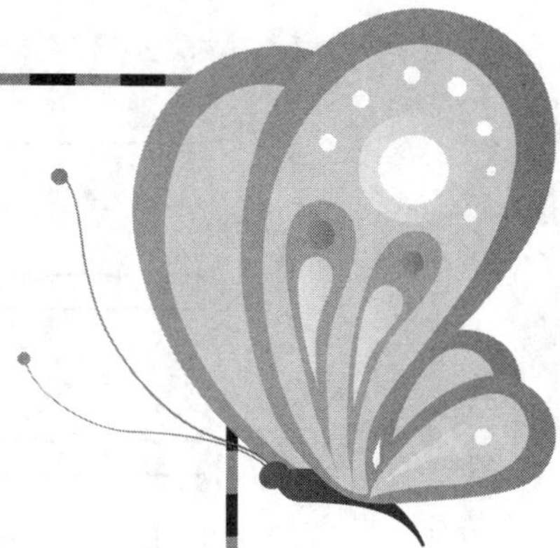

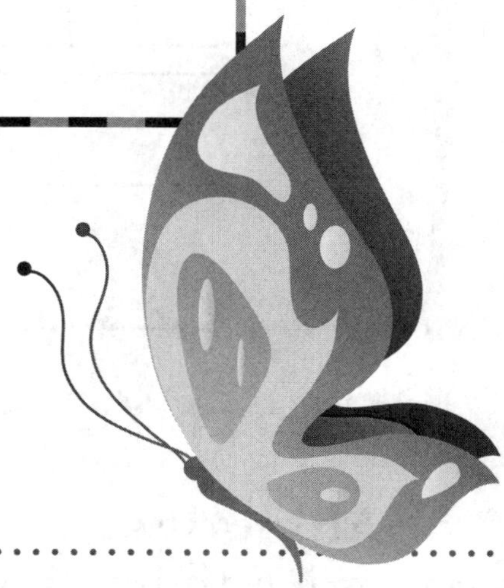

Printing Practice abc

Directions: Trace the sentence.

Butterflies are neat.

NAME: ______________________________

Directions: Think about butterflies. Add an adjective from the Word Bank to each of the words below.

Word Bank

sweet	patterned	two	cold
six	colorful	tiny	long

1. ______________________ wings
2. ______________________ legs
3. ______________________ eggs
4. ______________________ nectar
5. ______________________ winters

Boost Your Learning!

Adjectives give more description. They make things easier for the reader to picture.

Example
Butterflies have wings.

Butterflies have patterned wings.

NAME: ______________________________

Directions: Use editing symbols to correct the paragraph.

Editing Symbols

/ ⊙

Did you know That a butterfly goes through a big change? A butterfly lays an egg on a leaf When the egg hatches, it is A caterpillar. The caterpillar eats and eats. It grows and grows Then, it maKes a chrysalis. It stays inside for many days While it is inside, it changes. when it comes out, it is a butterfly.

Boost Your Learning!

Use the / symbol to make a word lowercase.

NAME: ____________________

Directions: Read the text. Draw a picture to match. Then, fill in the checklist.

Butterflies are a type of insect. They have wings that let them fly. Their wings have patterns. They fly to flowers. They sip the nectar. Butterflies are interesting!

Checklist ☑

- ❑ Sentences begin with capital letters.
- ❑ Sentences end with punctuation.
- ❑ There are spaces between words.

NAME: ______________________________

Directions: Place check marks in the circles that have to do with birds.

birds

- They have wings.
- They have feathers.
- Each bird has two legs.
- Insects crawl on the ground.
- They make nests.
- People have pets.
- They eat worms.

NAME: ______________________________

Drafting
Birds

Directions: Write about birds. Then, fill in the checklist.

Birds are ______________________________.

They have ______________________________

____.

____.

Birds are ______________________________.

Checklist ☑

- ☐ I have a topic sentence.
- ☐ I have a detail.
- ☐ I have a closing.

NAME: ______________________________

Directions: Think about describing birds. Add an adjective to each of the words below.

1. ______________________ wings
2. ______________________ legs
3. ______________________ eggs
4. ______________________ nest
5. ______________________ worm

Time to Improve!

Directions: Think of two different adjectives that you can use to describe a bird.

______________________ bird

______________________ bird

NAME: ______________________________

Directions: Use the Editing Symbols to correct the paragraph.

Editing Symbols

/ ⊙

Have you ever wished you could fly? Many birds can. They use their wings to soar high in the sky Their bones are hollow This makes them Light enough to fly. But not all birds can fly Birds like The penguin, ostrich, and emu cannot. They Do other things well.

NAME: ____________________________

Directions: Draw and write about a bird. Then, fill in the checklist.

Checklist ☑

- ☐ Sentences begin with capital letters.
- ☐ Sentences end with punctuation.
- ☐ There are spaces between the words.

NAME: ______________________________

Directions: Place check marks in the circles that have to do with the Statue of Liberty.

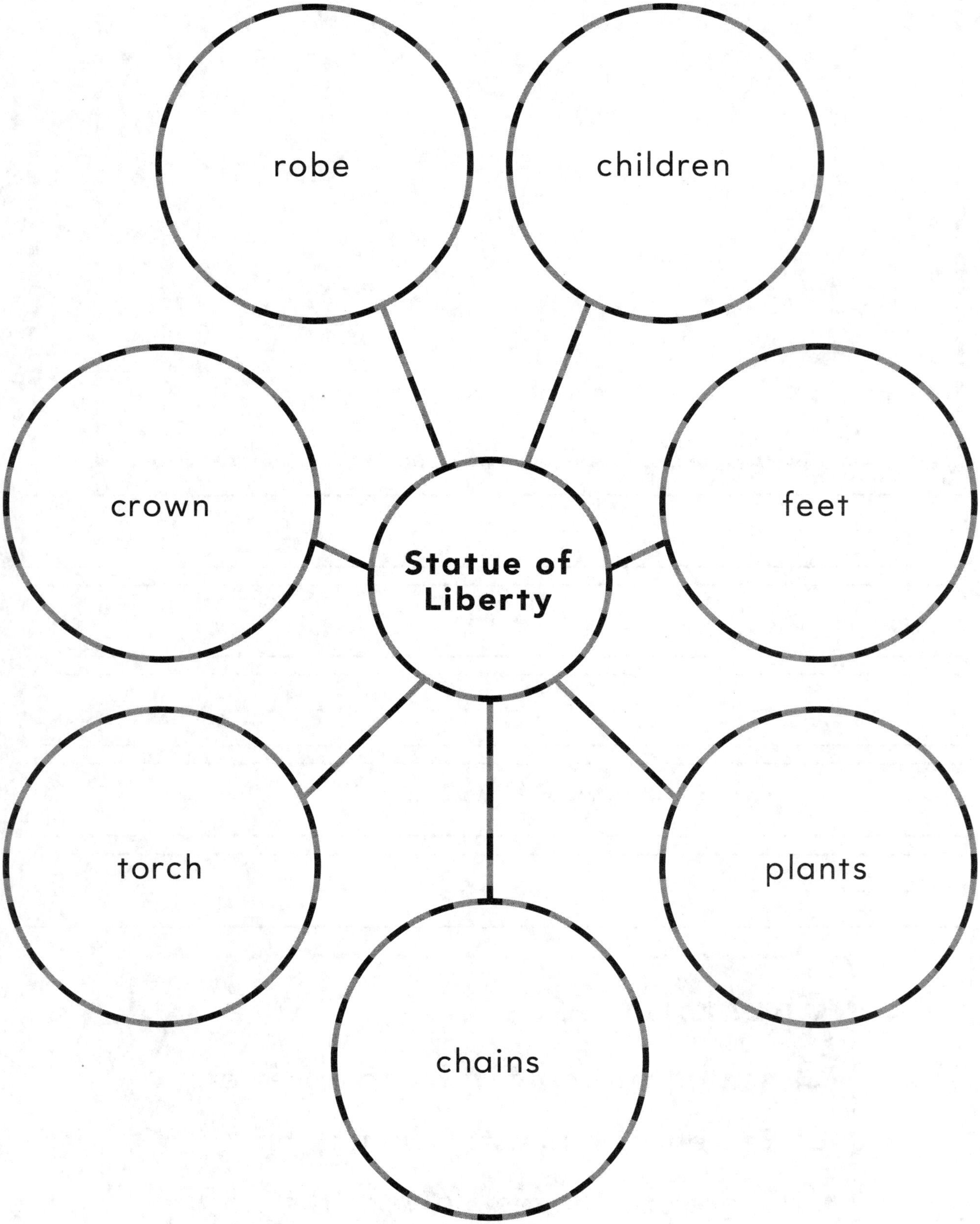

NAME: ____________________

Directions: Read the text. Then, underline each sentence in green, red, or blue.

Green:	**Red:**	**Blue:**
topic	detail	closure

The Statue of Liberty was a gift from France. She has a crown on her head. She has a torch in her hand. The Statue of Liberty is a symbol of freedom.

Printing Practice abc

Directions: Trace the words.

Statue of Liberty

NAME: ____

Directions: Read the paragraph. Then, follow the steps.

The Statue of Liberty is a symbol of freedom. She stands on a pedestal. The Statue of Liberty has a crown. The Statue of Liberty has a torch. The French word for statue is *statufier*. There is a tablet in her hand. There are chains on her feet. She is a reminder of the freedom in America.

Steps

1. Draw lines through sentences that are off topic.
2. Circle sentences that can be combined.

Boost Your Learning!

Sentences that tell about similar things can be combined.

Example
The pedestal is tall. The statue is tall.

The pedestal **and** statue are tall.

NAME: ______________________________

Directions: Underline the correct verb.

1. The Statue of Liberty (**is** or **was**) a symbol of freedom.
2. The Statue of Liberty (**has** or **had**) a crown.
3. The Statue of Liberty (**has** or **had**) a torch.
4. There (**is** or **was**) a tablet in her hand.
5. There (**is** or **was**) a chain on her feet.
6. She (**is** or **was**) a reminder of the freedom in America.

Boost Your Learning!

Use **is** and **has** when writing about the present. Use **was** and **had** when talking about the past.

NAME: ____________________

Drafting
The Flag

Directions: Write about flags. Then, fill in the checklist.

Flags are ____________________.

They have ____________________
____
____________________.

Flags are ____________________.

Checklist ☑

- ❑ I have a topic sentence.
- ❑ I have a detail.
- ❑ I have a closing.

NAME: ______________________________

Directions: Read the paragraph. Then, follow the steps.

The American flag represents America. Its colors are red, white, and blue. It has seven red stripes and six white stripes. The American flag also has a blue box with fifty stars in it. The German flag is black, red, and yellow. The flag is a symbol that helps us remember America.

Steps

1. Draw lines through sentences that are off topic.
2. Circle sentences that can be combined.

Time to Improve!

Directions: Combine the two sentences below.

The flag is called *Old Glory*. The flag is called the *Stars and Stripes*.

NAME: ______________________________

Directions: Circle the correct verb for each sentence.

1. Its colors (**are** or **were**) red, white, and blue.
2. It (**has** or **had**) seven red stripes and six white stripes.
3. The American flag also (**has** or **had**) a blue box with fifty stars in it.
4. The flag (**is** or **was**) a symbol that helps us remember America.

Time to Improve!

Directions: Rewrite this sentence in the present tense.

The American flag was a symbol of freedom.

____

____

NAME: ________________________

Directions: Draw and write about your country's flag. Include at least one fact. Then, fill in the checklist.

Checklist ☑

- ❑ Sentences begin with capital letters.
- ❑ Sentences end with punctuation.
- ❑ There are spaces between the words.

NAME: ____

Directions: Read about four ways to write an introduction sentence. Circle the one you like the best.

My Beach Vacation

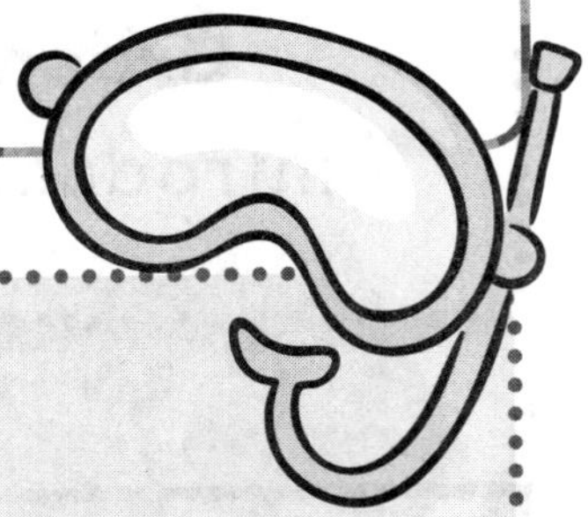

Statement: Tell something.

Last summer, my family took a vacation.

Question: Ask a question.

Do you know where I went last summer?

Interesting Fact: Tell an interesting related fact.

More people take vacations during the summer than any other time of year.

Onomatopoeia: Start with a sound effect.

Whoosh! The sound of ocean waves welcomed me to my beach vacation.

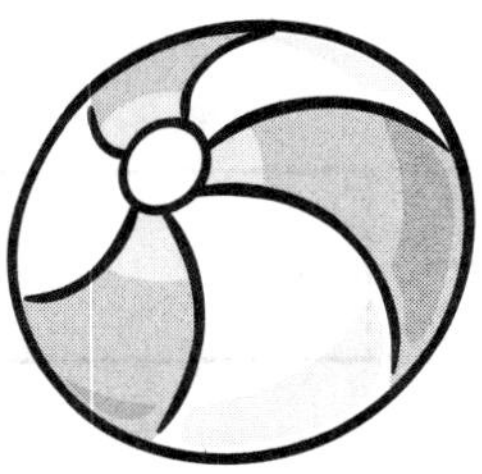

NAME: ______________________________

Directions: Add commas to the dates.

1. December 25 2017
2. August 2 2016
3. April 15 2018
4. February 14 2015
5. January 1 2017
6. October 31 2016

Remember!

A comma goes between the day and the year to keep the numbers separate.

July 4, 1776

NAME: ____________________

Directions: Read the text. Draw a picture to match. Then, fill in the checklist.

On June 12, 2015, my family went on a vacation. It was in Sunset Beach. First, we walked to the beach. Then, we played in the sand. Next, we played volleyball. It was the best vacation ever!

Checklist ☑

- ☐ Sentences begin with capital letters.
- ☐ Sentences end with punctuation.
- ☐ There are spaces between words.

NAME: ____

Directions: Think about a vacation. Complete the chart with notes about it.

Who? ______________________________

____

Where? ______________________________

When? ______________________________

Event 1 (Draw)	**Event 2** (Draw)

NAME: ______________________________

Editing : Vacation

Directions: Add commas (,) to the paragraph.

On July 1 2015, we flew on an airplane to Washington, DC. My family wanted to visit our country's capital and be there for the Fourth of July celebration. The Fourth of July honors the day we became a country. On July 4 1776, we declared we were free from Great Britain. We celebrate every year with fireworks. It was fun to see the fireworks, but it was a quick trip. We were back on a plane headed home on July 5 2015.

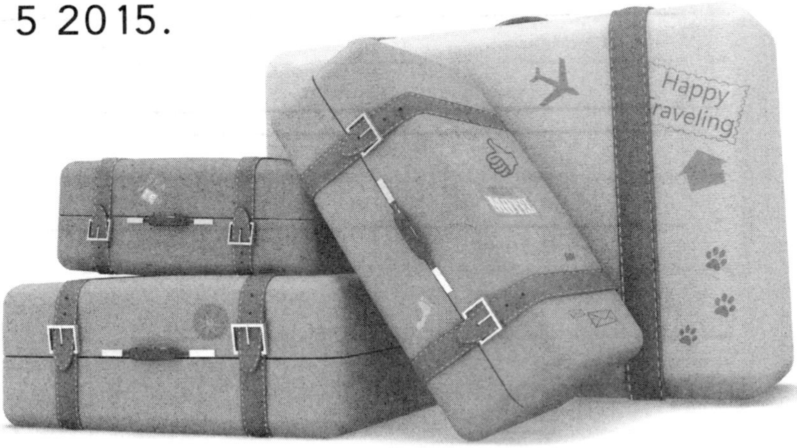

Time to Improve!

Directions: Write a date. Be sure to include a comma.

____

NAME: ______________________________

Directions: Draw and write about a vacation. Then, fill in the checklist.

Checklist ☑

- ☐ Sentences begin with capital letters.
- ☐ Sentences end with punctuation.
- ☐ There are spaces between the words.

ANSWER KEY

The activity pages that do not have specific answers to them are not included in this answer key. Students' answers will vary on these activity pages, so check that students are staying on task.

Week 1: School

Day 1 (page 14)

Students may place check marks next to all of them.

Day 2 (page 15)

Opinion: I like to go back to school.

Details: I get a new teacher. I get a new backpack. I see school friends again.

Closure: I look forward to going back to school.

Week 2: Teachers

Day 3 (page 21)

1. She teaches first grade.
2. The teacher helps the boy.
3. Her favorite subject is math.

Day 4 (page 22)

Students should insert a period at the end of each sentence.

Day 5 (page 23)

See Opinion Writing Rubric on page 200.

Week 3: Health Workers

Day 1 (page 24)

Students should circle the doctor, nurse, hospital, and stethoscope.

Day 2 (page 25)

Topic: Health workers take care of people.

Details: A doctor works in a hospital. He uses a stethoscope.

Closure: He helps people.

Day 3 (page 26)

1. she
2. he
3. he
4. she

Week 4: Safety Helpers

Day 1 (page 29)

Students should place check marks next to the circles with police, firefighters, help people, brave, and keep people safe.

Day 2 (page 30)

Safety helpers help people. A police **officer** works at a **police** station. A firefighter works at a **fire** station. These helpers **help** people.

Day 3 (page 31)

1. she
2. he

Day 4 (page 32)

Time to Improve: She

Day 5 (page 33)

See Informative/Explanatory Writing Rubric on page 201.

Week 5: Apples

Day 1 (page 34)

Students should circle the stem, leaf, seeds, and core.

Day 2 (page 35)

Topic: Fall is apple picking time!

Details: Apples grow on trees. Apples are red, green, and yellow. The middle is the core. It has the seeds.

Closure: Do you like apples?

Day 3 (page 36)

1. Apples can be red **or** yellow.
2. Apples have cores **and** seeds.
3. Apples can be sweet **or** sour.
4. Apples have stems **and** leaves.

Day 4 (page 37)

Students should insert a question mark at the end of each question.

Week 6: Pumpkins

Day 1 (page 39)

Students should circle the stem, rib, seeds, and pulp.

Day 2 (page 40)

Fall is **pumpkin** picking time! Pumpkins are orange. The outside has lines called **ribs**. The inside has **seeds** and **pulp**. Do you like pumpkins?

Day 3 (page 41)

1. Pumpkins can be big or small.
2. A pumpkin has pulp and seeds.
3. Pumpkins can be short or tall.

Day 4 (page 42)

1. What color is a pumpkin**?** **orange**
2. What are the lines on a pumpkin**?** **ribs**
3. When are pumpkins picked**?** **fall**
4. Where are the seeds**? inside**
5. What does a pumpkin grow on**? vine**

Day 5 (page 43)

See Informative/Explanatory Writing Rubric on page 201.

Week 7: Monsters

Day 1 (page 44)

Students should place check marks next to 2, 3, 4, and 5.

Day 2 (page 45)

Opinion: I think monsters are silly.

Details: They have crazy arms. They tell funny jokes.

Closure: I laugh when I see silly monsters.

ANSWER KEY *(cont.)*

Day 3 (page 46)

tiny, little, large, huge

The monster has a huge nose.

Day 4 (page 47)

1. October
2. July
3. December
4. January

Week 8: Candy

Day 3 (page 51)

disgusting, gross, yummy, delicious

Day 4 (page 52)

1. October
2. November
3. December

Time to Improve: My birthday is in November.

Day 5 (page 53)

See Opinion Writing Rubric on page 200.

Week 9: Soccer

Day 2 (page 55)

Introduction: My team had a soccer game at the park.

Events: When I got the ball, I aimed at the net. I kicked the winning goal. Everyone cheered for me.

Closure: It was a great game!

Day 3 (page 56)

Students should put an *X* next to these two sentences: I aimed at the net. We each got a trophy.

Day 4 (page 57)

1. I got a new soccer ball!
2. My best friend is on my team!
3. I scored a goal!
4. We won the game!
5. I got a trophy!

Week 10: Basketball

Day 3 (page 61)

1. My team is called the Ravens.
2. The score was 12 to 10.
3. We played hard so we could win.

Day 4 (page 62)

1. He scored!
2. A basketball is orange.
3. We are the champs!
4. Throw the ball in the basket to score.
5. She scored the winning basket.

Day 5 (page 63)

See Narrative Writing Rubric on page 202.

Week 11: Hibernating Animals

Day 2 (page 65)

Introduction: It was winter. I went for a walk to the pond with my mom.

Events: I did not see any ducks or turtles. Mom said the ducks fly south to stay warm. She told me the turtles bury themselves in the mud to hibernate.

Closure: We will see the ducks and turtles again in the spring.

Day 3 (page 66)

Pronouns: She, me, themselves, She, we

Day 4 (page 67)

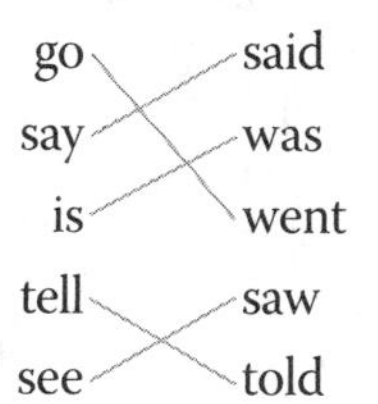

Week 12: Dressing for the Weather

Day 3 (page 71)

1. they
2. it
3. it

Time to Improve: It

Day 4 (page 72)

1. wore
2. was
3. could
4. dressed

Time to Improve: It was cold yesterday.

Day 5 (page 73)

See Narrative Writing Rubric on page 202.

Week 13: Winter Traditions

Day 1 (page 74)

Students should place check marks next to 1, 2, 4, and 5.

Day 2 (page 75)

Introduction: It is fun to bake gingerbread men.

Details: You get to decorate them. You also get to eat them.

Closure: I look forward to baking gingerbread men in the winter.

Day 4 (page 77)

1. Gingerbread men have raisin eyes.
2. Baking with my mom is the best!
3. There is a famous book about a gingerbread man.
4. Do you love the smell of ginger?
5. Gingerbread cookies are the best!

ANSWER KEY *(cont.)*

Week 14: Winter Celebrations

Day 4 (page 82)

1. Do you know the seven principles of Kwanzaa**?**
2. Hanukkah lasts seven days and eight nights**.**
3. We got candy from the piñata at the Las Posadas celebration**!**
4. Did you see the ice statues at the ice carnival**?**

Time to Improve: Where are the lights?

Day 5 (page 83)

See Opinion Writing Rubric on page 200.

Week 15: New Year

Day 1 (page 84)

Students should place check marks next to 1, 2, and 4.

Day 2 (page 85)

Opinion: My favorite celebration is New Year's Eve.

Details: I get to stay up late. I get to throw confetti in the air.

Closure: It is fun to ring in the new year.

Day 4 (page 87)

1. is
2. to
3. the
4. We
5. in

Week 16: Chinese New Year

Day 3 (page 91)

Students' answers may vary, but may include:

1. A colorful **dragon** dances.
2. We **get** red envelopes.
3. My **whole** family cleans.
4. We eat lots of **yummy** food.

Time to Improve: We greet our friends **by bringing them food.**

Day 4 (page 92)

1. is
2. has
3. are
4. They
5. We

Day 5 (page 93)

See Opinion Writing Rubric on page 200.

Week 17: Building Snowmen

Day 1 (page 94)

Students should place check marks next to 1, 2, 4, and 5.

Day 2 (page 95)

Opinion: Making a snowman is great!

Details: I get to play with snow. I get to name my snowman. I watch my snowman while I drink hot cocoa.

Closure: It is fun to build a snowman.

Day 3 (page 96)

Beginning Sentence—First, To begin

Middle Sentence—Then, Next

Ending Sentence—Finally, Lastly

Day 4 (page 97)

1. Roll big**,** medium**,** and small snowballs.
2. Put on a carrot nose**,** button eyes**,** and a coal mouth.
3. Add a scarf**,** a hat**,** and stick arms.
4. A snowman can be a boy**,** a girl**,** or a baby.

Week 18: Winter Sports

Day 3 (page 101)

Beginning sentence—First or To begin

Middle Sentence—Then, Next, Second, or Third

Ending Sentence—Finally or Lastly

Time to Improve: First or **To begin**, I carry the sled up the hill.

Day 4 (page 102)

1. I like to sled**,** ski**,** and skate.
2. It is fun to watch hockey**,** snowboarding**,** and skiing.
3. You need skis**,** poles**,** and boots.

Time to Improve: Winter has ice**,** wind**,** and snow.

Day 5 (page 103)

See Opinion Writing Rubric on page 200.

Week 19: Dr. Martin Luther King Jr.

Day 1 (page 104)

Students should place check marks in the circles: He was born on January 15, 1929; He wanted fairness, He was a minister; He wanted equality; and He died on April 4, 1968.

Day 2 (page 105)

Topic: Martin Luther King Jr. was an important leader.

Details: He planned boycotts. He gave speeches.

Closure: He was a great man.

Day 3 (page 106)

1. He married in 1953.
2. He planned boycotts.
3. He gave speeches.

Day 4 (page 107)

1. Michael King
2. Martin
3. Willie
4. Alfred

ANSWER KEY *(cont.)*

Week 20: George Washington

Day 1 (page 109)

Students should place check marks in the circles: Washington was born on February 22, 1732; He had many jobs; He helped write the Constitution; He was a president; and Washington died on December 14, 1799.

Day 2 (page 110)

George Washington was a great **leader** (or **president**). He lead an **army**. He became **president** (or **leader**).

Day 3 (page 111)

1. He
2. His
3. He
4. His

Time to Improve: He was a great leader.

Day 4 (page 112)

1. Washington
2. Martha
3. Washington
4. George
5. Washington

Day 5 (page 113)

See Informative/Explanatory Writing Rubric on page 201.

Week 21: Family

Day 2 (page 115)

Introduction: One time, I went on a picnic with my family.

Events: First, my mom packed a picnic lunch in a basket. Then, we went to Duck Park.

Closure: It was fun to spend time with my family.

Day 4 (page 117)

My family went for a bike ride. **First,** we got ready to go. Then, we rode to the park. **When** we got to the park, we fed the ducks**.** We had a lot of fun.

Week 22: Friends

Day 4 (page 122)

I had a play date with my friend, Max**.** First, we played with my toy cars. **Next,** we dug holes in the backyard. **We** had a great time together**.**

Time to Improve: A sentence ends with a period.

Day 5 (page 123)

See Narrative Writing Rubric on page 202.

Week 23: Pie

Day 1 (page 124)

Students should place check marks next to 1, 3, 4, and 5.

Day 2 (page 125)

Opinion: Apple pie is delicious.

Details: It has a yummy crust. It has crisp, fresh apples in it.

Closure: I always have room for apple pie!

Day 4 (page 127)

1. cake
2. rake
3. snake

Week 24: Pizza

Day 4 (page 132)

1. ice
2. dice
3. mice

Time to Improve: like, pizza

Day 5 (page 133)

See Opinion Writing Rubric on page 200.

Week 25: Airplanes

Day 2 (page 135)

Introduction: My grandparents and I went on a trip.

Events: First, we packed our bags. Then, we drove to the airport. Next, we flew on a plane. Next, we landed safely in New York.

Closure: We had a wonderful trip.

Day 3 (page 136)

Draw a line through sentences 2 and 5.

Day 4 (page 137)

1. an
2. a
3. a
4. an

Week 26: Kites

Day 3 (page 141)

Draw lines through sentences 1 and 4.

Time to Improve: They do not give details about flying a kite.

Day 4 (page 142)

1. I went to the beach and saw **a** man flying **a** kite.
2. The kite was the shape of **a** whale.
3. There was **a** ribbon tied on the kite string.
4. He made the kite do **an** exciting trick.
5. He said he had **an** eel-shaped kite, too.

Day 5 (page 143)

See Narrative Writing Rubric on page 202.

ANSWER KEY *(cont.)*

Week 27: Animals

Day 1 (page 144)

Students should circle the egg, nest, hen, baby chick, and hatch.

Day 2 (page 145)

Topic: The life cycle of a hen is neat.

Details: The mother hen lays an egg. She sits on the egg to keep it warm. The baby chick pecks its way out of the egg. It grows up to be a hen.

Closure: The life cycle starts again when the hen lays an egg.

Day 3 (page 146)

1. The mother hen lays an egg.
2. The mother hen sits on the egg to keep it warm.
3. The baby chick pecks its way out of the egg.
4. The baby chick grows up to be a hen.

Day 4 (page 147)

1. The mother **hen** <u>lays</u> an egg.
2. **She** <u>sits</u> on the egg.
3. The **baby chick** <u>pecks</u> its way out of the egg.
4. **It** <u>grows</u> up to be a hen.

Week 28: Plants

Day 1 (page 149)

Students should circle the water, sun, leaves, and stem.

Day 3 (page 151)

1. He
2. She
3. It

Time to Improve: plant, it; plants, they

Day 4 (page 152)

1. have
2. needs
3. grow

Time to Improve: grow

Day 5 (page 153)

See Informative/Explanatory Writing Rubric on page 201.

Week 29: Transportation

Day 2 (page 155)

Introduction: Last summer, my family and I went on vacation. We went on a boat.

Events: First, we packed our bags. Then, we drove to the boat. After we boarded, we sailed for three days.

Closure: It was a really fun trip!

Day 3 (page 156)

1. We flew for three hours, **and** then we were there.
2. She could travel by car **or** train.
3. It was fun flying **and** getting there so fast.

Day 4 (page 157)

Circle the following verbs in the paragraph—went, took, flew, picked, was

1. picked
2. made
3. went
4. was

Week 30: Technology

Day 3 (page 161)

1. You can type on a typewriter **and** on a computer.
2. Dial phones had cords, **so** you had to stay close to the phone.
3. You used to have to get up to change the channel on TV **because** there was not a remote control.

Time to Improve: My mom played outside when she was little, **because** there were no video games.

Day 4 (page 162)

My mom and I **walked** by a store. I **saw** something strange in the window. I **didn't** know what it was. My mom **said** it was a typewriter. She **said** that when she **went** to school that is what she **typed** on. I **thought** it was funny because I use a computer.

Time to Improve: I went to school today.

Day 5 (page 163)

See Narrative Writing Rubric on page 202.

Week 31: Butterflies

Day 1 (page 164)

Students should place check marks in the circles: Butterflies are insects; They have wings; They lay eggs; They begin as caterpillars; and They fly.

Day 2 (page 165)

Topic: Butterflies are a type of insect.

Details: They have wings that let them fly. Their wings have patterns. They fly to flowers. They sip the nectar.

Closure: Butterflies are interesting!

Day 4 (page 167)

Did you know **that** a butterfly goes through a big change? A butterfly lays an egg on a leaf**.** When the egg hatches, it is **a** caterpillar. The caterpillar eats and eats. It grows and grows**.** Then, it **makes** a chrysalis. It stays inside for many days**.** While it is inside, it changes. **When** it comes out, it is a butterfly.

ANSWER KEY *(cont.)*

Week 32: Birds

Day 1 (page 169)

Students should place check marks in the circles: Each bird has two legs; They have wings; They have feathers; They make nests; and They eat worms.

Day 4 (page 172)

Have you ever wished you could fly? Many birds can. They use their wings to soar high in the sky**.** Their bones are hollow**.** This makes them **light** enough to fly**.** But not all birds can fly**.** Birds like **the** penguin, ostrich, and emu cannot. They **do** other things well.

Day 5 (page 173)

See Informative/Explanatory Writing Rubric on page 201.

Week 33: The Statue of Liberty

Day 1 (page 174)

Students should place check marks in the circles with the crown, robe, feet, torch, and chains.

Day 2 (page 175)

Topic: The Statue of Liberty was a gift from France.

Details: She has a crown on her head. She has a torch in her hand.

Closure: The Statue of Liberty is a symbol of freedom.

Day 3 (page 176)

Students should draw a line through the following sentence: The French word for statue is *statufier*.

Students should circle these sentences: The Statue of Liberty has a crown. The Statue of Liberty has a torch. There is a tablet in her hand. There are chains on her feet.

Day 4 (page 177)

1. is
2. has
3. has
4. is
5. is
6. is

Week 34: The Flag

Day 1 (page 179)

Students should place check marks in the circles: Every country has one; They have colors; They have patterns; They have symbols; They wave in the air.

Day 3 (page 181)

Students should draw a line through the following sentence: The German flag is black, red, and yellow.

Students should circle these sentences: Its colors are red, white, and blue. It has seven red stripes and six white stripes.

Time to Improve: The flag is called *Old Glory* or the *Stars and Stripes*.

Day 4 (page 182)

1. are
2. has
3. has
4. is

Time to Improve: The American flag **is** a symbol of freedom.

Day 5 (page 183)

See Informative/Explanatory Writing Rubric on page 201.

Week 35: The Beach

Day 2 (page 185)

Introduction: On June 12, 2015, my family went on a vacation. It was in Sunset Beach.

Events: First, we walked to the beach. Then, we played in the sand. Next, we played volleyball.

Closure: It was the best vacation ever!

Day 4 (page 187)

1. December 25**,** 2017
2. August 2**,** 2016
3. April 15**,** 2018
4. February 14**,** 2015
5. January 1**,** 2017
6. October 31**,** 2016

Week 36: Vacation

Day 4 (page 192)

On July 1**,** 2015, we flew on an airplane to Washington, DC. My family wanted to visit our country's capital and be there for the Fourth of July celebration. The Fourth of July honors the day we became a country. On July 4**,** 1776, we declared we were free from Great Britain. We celebrate every year with fireworks. It was fun to see the fireworks, but it was a quick trip. We were back on a plane headed home on July 5**,** 2015.

Day 5 (page 193)

See Narrative Writing Rubric on page 202.

OPINION WRITING RUBRIC

Directions: Evaluate students' work in each category by circling one number in each row. Students have opportunities to score up to five points in each row and up to 15 points total.

	Exceptional Writing		Quality Writing		Developing Writing	
Focus and Organization	States a clear opinion. Includes lots of details. Includes a strong closing.		States an opinion. Includes at least one detail. Includes a closing.		States an unclear opinion. Includes few or unclear details. Does not include a closing.	
Points	5	4	3	2	1	0
Written Expression	Uses varied and interesting descriptive words. Maintains a consistent voice and uses a tone that supports meaning.		Uses some descriptive words. Maintains a consistent voice.		Uses a limited or an unvaried vocabulary. Provides an inconsistent voice.	
Points	5	4	3	2	1	0
Language Conventions	Sentences begin with capital letters. Sentences end in correct punctuation. Words in sentences have correct spacing between them.		Some sentences begin with capital letters. Some sentences end in correct punctuation. Most words in sentences have correct spacing between them.		Most sentences begin with lowercase letters. Sentences end in incorrect punctuation, or no punctuation is used. Words have incorrect spacing between them.	
Points	5	4	3	2	1	0

Total Points: ____________________

INFORMATIVE/EXPLANATORY WRITING RUBRIC

Directions: Evaluate students' work in each category by circling one number in each row. Students have opportunities to score up to five points in each row and up to 15 points total.

	Exceptional Writing		Quality Writing		Developing Writing	
Focus and Organization	States a clear topic sentence. Includes lots of details. Includes a strong closing.		States a topic sentence. Includes at least one detail. Includes a closing.		States an unclear topic sentence. Includes few or unclear details. Does not include a closing.	
Points	5	4	3	2	1	0
Written Expression	Uses varied and interesting descriptive words. Maintains a consistent voice and uses a tone that supports meaning.		Uses some descriptive words. Maintains a consistent voice.		Uses a limited or an unvaried vocabulary. Provides an inconsistent voice.	
Points	5	4	3	2	1	0
Language Conventions	Sentences begin with capital letters. Sentences end in correct punctuation. Words in sentences have correct spacing between them.		Some sentences begin with capital letters. Some sentences end in correct punctuation. Most words in sentences have correct spacing between them.		Most sentences begin with lowercase letters. Sentences end in incorrect punctuation, or no punctuation is used. Words have incorrect spacing between them.	
Points	5	4	3	2	1	0

Total Points: ____________________

NARRATIVE WRITING RUBRIC

Directions: Evaluate students' work in each category by circling one number in each row. Students have opportunities to score up to five points in each row and up to 15 points total.

	Exceptional Writing		Quality Writing		Developing Writing	
Focus and Organization	States a clear introduction. Includes lots of events. Includes a strong closing.		States an introduction. Includes at least one event. Includes a closing.		States an unclear introduction. Includes few or unclear events. Does not include a closing.	
Points	5	4	3	2	1	0
Written Expression	Uses varied and interesting descriptive words. Maintains a consistent voice and uses a tone that supports meaning.		Uses some descriptive words. Maintains a consistent voice.		Uses a limited or an unvaried vocabulary. Provides an inconsistent voice.	
Points	5	4	3	2	1	0
Language Conventions	Sentences begin with capital letters. Sentences end in correct punctuation. Words in sentences have correct spacing between them.		Some sentences begin with capital letters. Some sentences end in correct punctuation. Most words in sentences have correct spacing between them.		Most sentences begin with lowercase letters. Sentences end in incorrect punctuation, or no punctuation is used. Words have incorrect spacing between them.	
Points	5	4	3	2	1	0

Total Points: ____________________

OPINION WRITING ANALYSIS

Directions: Record each student's rubric scores (page 200) in the appropriate columns. Add the totals every two weeks and record the sums in the Total Scores column. You can view: (1) which students are not understanding the opinion genre and (2) how students progress after multiple encounters with the opinion genre.

	Week 2	Week 8	Week 14	Week 16	Week 18	Week 24	Total Scores
Student Name							
Average Classroom Score							

INFORMATIVE/EXPLANATORY WRITING ANALYSIS

Directions: Record each student's rubric score (page 201) in the appropriate columns. Add the totals every two weeks and record the sums in the Total Scores column. You can view: (1) which students are not understanding the informative/explanatory genre and (2) how students progress after multiple encounters with the informative/explanatory genre.

	Week 4	Week 6	Week 20	Week 28	Week 32	Week 34	Total Scores
Student Name							
Average Classroom Score							

NARRATIVE WRITING ANALYSIS

Directions: Record each student's rubric score (page 202) in the appropriate columns. Add the totals every two weeks and record the sums in the Total Scores column. You can view: (1) which students are not understanding the narrative genre and (2) how students progress after multiple encounters with the narrative genre.

	Week 10	Week 12	Week 22	Week 26	Week 30	Week 36	Total Scores
Student Name							
Average Classroom Score							

THE WRITING PROCESS

STEP 1: **PREWRITING**

Think about the topic.
Brainstorm ideas.

STEP 2: **DRAFTING**

Use your ideas to write a draft.
Don't worry about errors.

STEP 3: **REVISING**

Read your draft. Think about the vocabulary. Think about the organization. Make changes to improve your writing.

STEP 4: **EDITING**

Reread your draft. Check for errors in spelling, punctuation, and grammar.

STEP 5: **PUBLISHING**

Create a final draft. Be sure to use your best printing.

EDITING MARKS

Editing Marks	Symbol Names	Example
≡	capitalization symbol	david ate grapes. (≡ under d)
/	lowercase symbol	My mother hugged Me. (/ through M)
⊙	insert period symbol	The clouds are in the sky⊙
sp◯	check spelling symbol	I laffed at the story. (sp, laffed circled)
∽	transpose symbol	How you are? (you and are looped)
^	insert symbol	Would you ^please pass the pizza?
^,	insert comma symbol	I have cats, dogs^, and goldfish.
“ ” (^ ^)	insert quotations symbol	“That is amazing,” she shouted.
ℓ	deletion symbol	Will you ~~call~~ call me?
#	add space symbol	I run to#the tree.

OPINION WRITING TIPS

INFORMATIVE/EXPLANATORY WRITING TIPS

1. Choose a topic.
2. Write a strong topic sentence.
3. Write facts about the topic.
4. Finish with a strong statement about the topic.
5. Check for correct spelling and punctuation.

NARRATIVE WRITING TIPS

Write a topic sentence that tells what your story is about.

Write in a logical order with a beginning, a middle, and an end.

Include characters.

Join the sentences with the words *first*, *next*, *then*, and *finally*.

Check for correct spelling and punctuation.

Use lots of details and sensory words.

Opinion Writing

Informative/Explanatory Writing

Narrative Writing

PEER/SELF-EDITING CHECKLIST

Directions: Place a check mark in front of each item as you check it.

The writing has . . .

- ❑ an opinion or topic stated
- ❑ an engaging beginning
- ❑ details about the opinion or topic
- ❑ a strong conclusion
- ❑ a logical order
- ❑ interesting words
- ❑ capital letters
- ❑ correct spelling
- ❑ correct punctuation

DIGITAL RESOURCES

Accessing the Digital Resources

The digital resources can be downloaded by following these steps:

1. Go to **www.tcmpub.com/digital**
2. Sign in or create an account.
3. Click **Redeem Content** and enter the ISBN number, located on page 2 and the back cover, into the appropriate field on the website.
4. Respond to the prompts using the book to view your account and available digital content.
5. Choose the digital resources you would like to download. You can download all the files at once, or you can download a specific group of files.

Please note: Some files provided for download have large file sizes. Download times for these larger files will vary based on your download speed.

CONTENTS OF THE DIGITAL RESOURCES

Teacher Resources

- Informative/Explanatory Writing Analysis
- Narrative Writing Analysis
- Opinion Writing Analysis
- Writing Rubric
- Writing Signs

Student Resources

- Peer/Self-Editing Checklist
- Editing Marks
- Practice Pages
- The Writing Process
- Writing Prompts
- Writing Tips

NOTES

